The Spokesman
What Price Austerity?
Edited by Tony Simpson

**Published by Spokesman for the
Bertrand Russell Peace Foundation**

UK)

Spokesman 110   2010

on requ...

A CIP catalogue record
for this book is available
from the British Library

Published by the
Bertrand Russell Peace
Foundation Ltd.,
Russell House
Bulwell Lane
Nottingham NG6 0BT
England
Tel. 0115 9784504
email:
elfeuro@compuserve.com
www.spokesmanbooks.com
www.russfound.org

CONTENTS

FSC
Mixed Sources
Product group from well-managed
forests and other controlled sources

Cert no. SGS-COC-006541
www.fsc.org
© 1996 Forest Stewardship Council

ISSN 1367 7748   Printed by the Russell Press Ltd., Nottingham, UK   ISBN 978 0 85124 785 4

GMB@WORK

GROWTH, ACCOUNTABILITY AND DEMOCRACY IN GMB

Total GMB membership has grown by 15% in real terms over the previous five years following the adoption of the GMB@Work national organising strategy in 2005.

GMB emerged from a deep financial crisis and the threat of merger in 2004/5 with a new leadership but fewer officers and resources than at any other time. Yet by spending less and asking more of GMB Workplace Organisers GMB has turned around decades of membership and financial decline.

GMB developed a single set of 38 policies and organising approaches simply based on a common understanding of what works and what doesn't. These have been adopted and implemented in all GMB Regions and GMB Sections. But the GMB@Work strategy has five fundamental organising principles which we promote to all GMB Officials and GMB Workplace Organisers.

GMB's growth rate and the GMB@Work strategy have begun to fundamentally change the union. Four out of five members are now service workers, almost half are women, officials no longer sit on the CEC, sections have been reduced from eight to three and we have returned to an annual GMB Congress—all to focus on the core truth: that a growing GMB delivers for GMB members while a shrinking GMB lets members down.

GMB@WORK STRATEGY

1. The workplace is the building block of GMB. It is at work, rather than in the community or in the media, that working people are most able to build the collective solidarity they need to tackle the injustice and inequality they face head on.

2. Each GMB workplace is organised as if a ballot for industrial action was due. GMB need GMB members to be match fit and ready, but we also need our organisation in each workplace to be democratic, transparent and accountable every day.

3. The employers have different interests than GMB members. It is GMB members' employers who are the cause of most of GMB members' problems at work and the Union's job is to stand up for and promote members' interests, not to bury them in partnership agreements.

4. It is the process of industrial relations that builds a union. People don't join unions out of gratitude for what was done in the past but out of fear and anger for the present and hope for the future.

5. People are strongest when they organise themselves. GMB members are encouraged to find their own solutions to the problems they face. GMB members in each workplace must have the power and authority they need to make decisions and officers must stop doing for members what they can do for themselves. Workplace democracy and organising must co-exist.

JOIN GMB ONLINE AT WWW.GMB.ORG.UK

Editorial

What price austerity?

Whilst still in opposition, in August 2009, the then Shadow Chancellor, George Osborne, argued for what he called 'progressive' and 'fundamental' reform of public services. The alternative, according to the Chancellor in waiting, was 'deep cuts in the quality of those services'. Praying in aid Tony Blair and Alan Milburn, who were by then advocating something similar, he said that what was true 'in the years of plenty' was doubly true in an age of austerity.

Now installed, Chancellor Osborne has set about his austere task with a will. As the comprehensive spending review looks to slice further tens of billions from departmental budgets, the cuts are already scything through public services round the country. Local government workers in their tens of thousands have received Section 118 redundancy notices, as have their counterparts in the Civil Service and sundry quangos. Public service, and all its outworks, is being chopped hard. Osborne shows little awareness of how adversely his cuts impact the private sector. The likelihood of a double-dip recession, not to say a full-blown slump, seems to worry him hardly at all.

It does, however, worry more responsible, and experienced, commentators. Joseph Stiglitz, for example, the Nobel Prize-winning economist, warns there is a 'wave of austerity' building throughout Europe (see box). He makes the compelling point that, as so many countries cut back on spending prematurely, 'global aggregate demand will be lowered and growth will slow – even perhaps leading to a double-dip recession'. He acknowledges that America may have caused the global recession, 'but Europe is now responding in kind'. 'The eurozone needs better co-operation,' says Professor Stiglitz, 'not just the kind that merely enforces budget rules, but co-operation that also ensures Europe remains at full employment, and that when countries experience large adverse shocks, they get help from others'.

The Trade Union Congress, when it gathered in Manchester, met the wave of austerity head-on. It exposed the Coalition's bogus argument about the overriding necessity to reduce the deficit, which provides cover for Chancellor Osborne to wield the axe in his spurious cause of 'progressive reform'. We print below the excellent briefing on this question which has been issued by the Public and Commercial Services Union (PCS), whose General Secretary, Mark Serwotka, explained to Congress why not a single job has to be lost, not a single penny should be cut in public spending. As he says, there is an alternative.

Wave of austerity

'To make up for the losses of these vital tools for adjustment, the eurozone should have created a fund to help those facing adverse problems. The US is a 'single currency' area, but when California has a problem, and its unemployment rate goes up, a large part of the costs are borne by the federal government. Europe has no way of helping countries facing severe difficulties ... The worry is that there is a wave of austerity building througout Europe (... even hitting America's shores). As so many countries cut back on spending prematurely, global aggregate demand will be lowered and growth will slow – even perhaps leading to a double-dip recession.

America may have caused the global recession, but Europe is now responding in kind. The eurozone needs better co-operation – not just the kind that merely enforces budget rules, but co-operation that also ensures that Europe remains at full employment, and that when countries experience large adverse shocks, they get help from others. Europe created a solidarity fund to help new entrants into the European Union, most of whom were poorer than all the others. But it failed to create a solidarity fund to help any part of the eurozone that was facing stress. Without some such fund, the future prospects of the euro are bleak ...'

Joseph Stiglitz, *in the Afterword to the new edition of his book* Freefall: America, Free Markets, and the Sinking of the World Economy *(Penguin, £9.99)*

* * *

Labour's new Leader

Ed Miliband was not supposed to win the election to become Leader of the Labour Party. Most of the remaining Blairite MPs and some MEPs, and quite a lot of money, piled in behind brother David. It was the votes of individual trade unionists that swung it for Ed. In so doing, they and their unions have helped to open up a little political space, which is as uncommon as it is welcome in modern British politics. Into that space, whilst it's there, we extend Stuart Holland's reflections on public ownership and Old Labour. With an insider's grasp of the detail, reaching back to the 1960s, Stuart challenges the stereotyping of 'Old' Labour as 'outdated nationalisation' and 'civil servants running industry' by showing that Labour's Programmes from 1973 to 1983 were based on French and Italian industrial policy; that the Party never proposed to 'nationalise the top 25 companies', and that its proposals for selective public ownership through a National Enterprise Board were widely endorsed within the Party. He shows how France has developed its high-speed rail network, retained many of its own manufacturing industries, and, so far, avoided Three Mile Island-type accidents within its nuclear industry as a consequence, in significant measure, of planning agreements with leading firms including those which were publicly owned. These lessons remain pertinent, notwithstanding Ed's avowal that 'we changed Clause 4' and 'we were right to do so'.

The new Leader's arrival has also opened up some much needed space on foreign policy. Ed Miliband put it this way in his Conference speech: 'this generation wants to change our foreign policy so that it's always based on values, not just alliances'. During the campaign, he was refreshingly explicit. He told the BBC Question Time audience:

> 'There is something that we have got to get to grips with in our foreign policy, which is our relationship with the USA. Unless we get to grips with that, and understand the deeper lessons of Iraq, then the danger is we make the same mistake in the future.'

If the Labour Party can, indeed, learn that deeper lesson, then something will truly have moved.

* * *

Deception and cover-up

'Bush wanted to remove Saddam, through military action, justified by the conjunction of terrorism and WMD. But the intelligence and facts were being fixed around the policy.'

Sir Richard Dearlove
Head of the Secret Intelligence Service
Prime Minister's meeting on Iraq, Downing Street, 23 July 2002

'Deception' is one of the part titles of Brian Jones' new book, *Failing Intelligence*, about which he writes elsewhere in this issue. Dr Jones thinks the unthinkable. He writes that Dearlove's mention of fixing 'may have been a suggestion that London would have to do the same' (page 72).

The Downing Street Memo, which contained Dearlove's candid remarks quoted above, spawned an enormous upsurge of activity and research in the United States. There, in May 2005, the After Downing Street coalition sought to expose the lies that had launched the war on Iraq, and hold accountable its architects, including through 'censure and impeachment'. Congressman John Conyers took up the campaign with a passion.

May 2005 was, of course, the month of Blair's last election. The Downing Street Memo had been leaked 'during his race', as President Bush complained, thus avoiding questions about the difficult issues that were raised by the document. Nor did Mr Blair give answers that were any straighter. A series of devastating leaks had charted his Government's preparations for his own key meeting with President Bush at Crawford, in April 2002. There, it seems, he pledged the United Kingdom to Bush's coming war. But the PM was then able to brazen his way through. Now, Tony Blair dare not sign copies of his memoir for fear of citizen's arrest.

The briefing paper for the meeting in Downing Street on 23 July 2002, in addition to the minute of the meeting itself*, was also leaked in 2005. Dr Jones had not been aware of the Downing Street meeting when he and his colleagues were insisting, unsuccessfully as it turned out, on accurate intelligence in the Government's Dossier, *Iraq's Weapons of Mass Destruction: The Assessment of the British Government*. Only now, whilst a fifth official inquiry is still in train in Britain, has the deception and subsequent cover-up been exposed in some detail. Dr Jones has pieced together the evidence, and written a telling indictment. What will be the response?

Tony Simpson

* See *The Dodgiest Dossier*, www.spokesmanbooks.com

Long forgotten?

'… Mr Clegg hopes that forcing banks to disclose – in pay bands – all bonuses over £1m will force them to show more restraint, but even on this score he will be disappointed in the short term. The Treasury has failed to table the secondary legislation needed to force banks to include the details in their annual reports in March: by the time the legal instrument is in place, the bonus season may be long forgotten.'

Financial Times, 22 September 2010

Not a single job has to be lost

Mark Serwotka

The General Secretary of the Public and Commercial Services union addressed the Trade Union Congress in Manchester on 13 September 2010. His union's analysis of the situation in Britain, entitled 'There is an alternative', follows.

We have already heard that the attacks that we are about to face will be the biggest that any of us will ever have experienced. Not only attacks on welfare, attacks on pensions, attacks on jobs, attacks on pay, a mass of privatisation, in fact if these cuts go unchallenged we will see whole parts of the communities where our members live devastated and laid to waste. Let's be clear, these attacks will not just affect public sector workers, they will also affect public service users and members in the private sector. For every 600,000 jobs lost in the public sector there will be up to 700,000 jobs lost in the private sector.

So let's not fall for the nonsense – the divide here is not public versus private, the divide is the haves against the have nots. We are speaking up for the have nots. Let us not take lectures from millionaires who have spent their lives in a bubble of privilege about lifestyle choices of welfare scroungers. The real scroungers are the rich who avoid paying their taxes in this country – to the extent of £120bn. These are the scroungers who should be held to account. Benefit fraud is reckoned to be £1bn. Tax avoidance and evasion is £120bn. That is why we have to be bold in our arguments.

We should not accept that a single job has to be lost, not a single penny should be cut in public spending, because there is an alternative; and if we don't advocate the alternative we will start choosing between which are the deserving jobs and which are the ones that have to go. The alternative is clear. The alternative is to collect the taxes that are due, and the alternative is to grow our way out of recession. Currently our deficit is 52 per cent of gross domestic product. For more than 50 years in this country that deficit was over 100 per cent – twice as bad as it is now – yet we built a National Health Service, comprehensive education and council houses. Now is the time to invest in transport and housing.

I hope we all agree that we should not accept any cuts whatsoever. But the government are unlikely to be persuaded, so we have to be clear – industrial action is inevitable unless the government are prepared to change direction. The responsibility on this movement, on every trade union represented, is not to wait. It is to start planning now. Getting the representatives to meet in every town and every city. Set up the community based campaigning with service users who will support us if we stand up to defend their services.

If we have to take industrial action the onus is on us to make that action as effective as possible to ensure we can win. That is why we have to learn some of the lessons of history. Those lessons are quite clear – when we stand together we are more effective. When eight unions stood and balloted against the cuts threatened to our pensions by the Labour Government, we didn't even have to take the action before we got an acceptable settlement. If all public sector unions and our colleagues in the private sector stand together not only can we win but we can also offer hope and inspiration to people who are looking to us to stand up for them, to stand up for their public services, and to reject the politics of division and greed from the rich, the famous and this government.

ASLEF the train drivers' union

www.aslef.org.uk

'To cut: to lower, reduce, diminish, or curtail.'

This the ConDem vision for our public services.

Let's not criticise. Let's organise.

Keith Norman
General Secretary

Alan Donnelly
President

There is an alternative

PCS

The Public and Commercial Services Union makes the case against cuts in public spending.

Foreword

We are told there is a deficit crisis in the United Kingdom. We are told that we are spending beyond our means. We are told that the solution to this deficit crisis is to cut public spending.

Public spending is an investment, not a debt. Public servants – the vast majority of whom are low paid – deliver vital services to our communities. The campaign of vilification against public services is motivated by a desire to cut and privatise these vital services. The reality is that there does not need to be a single penny taken away from any public service, or a single job lost.

The deficit is due to the recession, which has reduced revenues as less people are in work and are therefore spending less. At the same time, government expenditure has increased as more people are without work and are entitled to benefits. If the government cuts more jobs this will only exacerbate the deficit crisis – more people will be unemployed and there will be less revenue.

The answer to the crisis is, therefore, to create jobs, not cut them. Currently there are less than 500,000 vacancies, while 2.5 million people are unemployed. 'Getting tough' on welfare will not work since there are not the jobs available. It will simply cause more misery – which is the only possible outcome of the coalition government's policies. This is why we must resist this government's policy of savage cuts, and reject their flawed arguments. We need a new economic strategy based on public investment, job creation, and tax justice.

Over the coming months we need to win the arguments for this alternative and then force government to implement it. Otherwise

What Price Austerity?

our members and our communities could face years of misery. This short article spells out the compelling case against cuts, and for a new vision.

Mark Serwotka, General Secretary
Janice Godrich, President

* * *

The government's cuts strategy
– and why it's wrong

Firstly, we need to get the 'debt crisis' in perspective. The table below shows UK debt relative to other major economies.

Debt as % of GDP

Country	Debt as % of GDP
Japan	~200
US	~88
France	~82
Germany	~83
UK	~52

(bar chart, horizontal axis 0, 50, 100, 150, 200)

From 1918 to 1961 the UK national debt was over 100% of gross domestic product. During that period the government introduced the welfare state, the National Health Service, state pensions, comprehensive education, built millions of council houses, and nationalised a range of industries. The public sector grew and there was economic growth.

Today, the coalition government wants to turn back the clock. It is set on dismantling the NHS and comprehensive education, and it is attacking the welfare state. It is not doing this because the country is on the verge of economic collapse, it is doing it because it is ideologically opposed to public services and the welfare state, and committed to handing over more of our public assets to big business.

Cutting public sector jobs will increase unemployment. This would mean increased costs for government in benefit payments and lost tax revenue. If people's incomes are taken away, or cut through pay freezes, they will spend less. Less consumer spending means cuts in the private sector, and lower VAT revenues.

Internal analysis by HM Treasury proves this to be the case. Leaked documents estimated that, over the next six years, 600,000 public sector jobs would be cut, and 700,000 private sector jobs would also be lost – based on the current government's policies. Job cuts are therefore counterproductive. Mass job cuts would worsen the economic situation by reducing demand in the economy, and providing less tax revenue.

The government claims it can make cuts of between 25 per cent and 40 per cent, and still 'protect frontline public services'. This is impossible – not just because 'frontline services' are being cut, but because services rely on 'back office' support staff. For example, cutting support staff such as NHS cleaners has meant an increase in healthcare acquired infections, costing the NHS £1 billion. All public services require tax revenues to fund them, yet HM Revenue & Customs has cut 25,000 staff in recent years, which has led to uncollected tax at record levels and a growing tax gap.

The experience of Ireland

Ireland shows how cutting public spending can damage the economy. The crisis in Ireland was caused by the collapse of its banking sector. The massive cuts in spending and public sector pay that followed have increased unemployment and sapped demand, causing the economy to shrink further. Because of this, Ireland is now considered more at risk of sovereign default than before it started making cuts. Historical research clearly demonstrates that budget cuts actually provoke increases in the national debt by damaging the economy.

The impact is likely to be highly divisive, too. There is evidence of this already in the UK. In areas where public sector workers have already been laid off, retail sales have fallen faster than the UK average. In nations and regions where public sector workers make up a high proportion of the workforce, major public sector cuts could destroy local economies. Any attack on the public sector will also disproportionately affect women, as 68 per cent of the public sector workforce is female. The public sector also has a much better record of employing disabled workers.

The global race to cut labour costs is central to the economic collapse we have seen around the world. Squeezed consumers are defaulting on mortgages and personal debts, and are less able to spend in the economy. In the UK, the value of wages has declined from nearly 65 per cent of GDP in the mid-1970s to 55% today. Over the same period, the rate of corporate profit has increased from 13% to 21%. It is no coincidence that in this period trade union rights were severely restricted, large swathes of the economy privatised, markets deregulated and corporation tax slashed.

There is an urgent need to rebalance the economy in the interests of people over big business.

Economic growth and public investment

Investing in public services is the solution to the deficit crisis. Instead of cutting jobs, we should be creating them. Jobs are not created by bullying people on benefits into jobs that don't exist. Instead there are several areas where public sector jobs urgently need to be created.

It has been estimated that over a million 'climate jobs' could be created if the government was serious about tackling both climate change and unemployment – these would include areas such as housing, renewable energy, and public transport investment, including high speed rail, bus networks, and electric car manufacture.

Today, there are 1.8 million families (representing over 5 million people) on council house waiting lists. There is an urgent need to build affordable housing for these people, which would also help reduce housing benefit payments.

The UK lags behind much of the rest of Europe in the development of a high-speed rail network, which would have the potential to create thousands of jobs and reduce carbon emissions by shifting passengers and freight away from road and air travel. Much of the country outside of London also needs huge investment in bus services – and, just as we should invest in electric car technology, we should also invest in electric buses and tram networks.

Only 2.2% of UK energy comes from renewable sources, compared with 8.9% in Germany, 11% in France, and an impressive 44.4% in Sweden. If we are committed to tackling climate change and ensuring domestic energy security there needs to be investment in renewable energy technology.

All of these industries would generate revenue – people are billed for electricity, buy tickets to travel on public transport, and pay rent for council housing. Research by Richard Murphy (of Tax Research) has shown that the state recoups 92% of the cost of creating new public sector jobs – through lower benefit payments and increased tax revenues.

The banks

We should never forget that it was the banking sector that caused the recession, and is ultimately responsible for the huge debts that the UK has amassed. Despite causing the crisis, the banking sector has escaped any significant regulation, and bankers are again awarding themselves huge bonuses.

The table below clearly shows how UK debt accelerated after the banking crisis in 2008.

Government debt as % of GDP

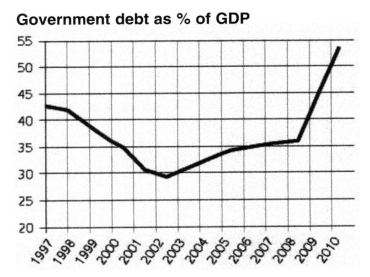

As a result of the UK government's £1.3 trillion bailout to the financial sector, the Government still owns over £850 billion in bank assets. This figure is roughly equal to the total UK debt.

The UK has an 84% stake in the Royal Bank of Scotland (RBS) and a 41% stake in Lloyds TSB. In addition, the state also owns Northern Rock and Bradford & Bingley. Under public ownership and control these assets could yield significant annual income to the Government, which could be used to meet social needs and tackle financial exclusion.

The case against privatisation

As a result of the Government's agenda to slash the public sector, privatisation, outsourcing and the Private Finance Initiative (PFI) are a fast growing threat to civil and public services despite the many performance failures of past privatisations. Privatisation is no solution to the national debt. Evidence confirms that, after transfer to the private sector, the terms and conditions of workers are worse than before, the public sector loses any revenue stream while ultimately keeping the risk, and services to the public decline or cost more:

- In the Department of Work and Pensions, welfare is now described as 'an annual multi-billion pound market' and, despite the department's own research showing that Jobcentre staff outperform the private sector in helping people back to work, all contracts for welfare private finance programmes are now outsourced.
- Qinetiq was a company formed from the privatisation of the Defence Evaluation and Research Agency (DERA). In 2007, the 10 most senior managers gained £107.5m on a total investment of £540,000 in the company's shares. The return of 19,990 per cent on their investment was described as 'excessive' by the National Audit Office. In 2009, Qinetiq offered its staff a pay freeze.
- Although the economic downturn has led to a drying up of bank finance for PFI projects, the government has got round this by funnelling public funds – through the Treasury's Infrastructure Finance Unit – to state owned banks who then loan finance to PFI consortia (which then claim inflated returns to government for the next thirty years, greatly exceeding the money given to them). The journalist and anti-privatisation activist, George Monbiot, observed, 'the Private Finance Initiative no longer requires much private finance or initiative'.

Public services were won by trade union struggles in an effort to establish the basis of a civilised society. Driven by the desire for maximum profits, the private sector fails to provide effective and efficient public services.

Tax justice

Addressing the 'tax gap' is a vital part of tackling the deficit. Figures produced for PCS by the Tax Justice Network show that £25 billion is lost annually in tax avoidance and a further £70 billion in tax evasion by large companies and wealthy individuals. An additional £26 billion is going uncollected. Therefore PCS estimates the total annual tax gap at over £120 billion (more than three-quarters of the annual deficit!). It is not just PCS calculating this; leaked Treasury documents, in 2006, estimated the tax gap at between £97 and £150 billion.

If we compare the PCS estimate of the tax gap with the Department of Work and Pensions estimate of benefit fraud, we can see that benefit fraud is less than one per cent of the total lost in the tax gap (see diagram below).

Employing more staff at HM Revenue & Customs would enable more tax to be collected, more investigations to take place, and evasion reduced. Compliance officers in HMRC bring in over £658,000 in revenue per employee.

Debt as % of GDP

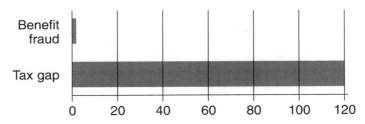

If the modest Robin Hood tax – a 0.05 per cent tax on global financial transactions – was applied to UK financial institutions, it would raise an estimated £20-30bn per year. This alone would reduce the annual deficit by between 12.5 per cent and 20 per cent. Closing the tax gap, as part of overall economic strategy, would negate the need for devastating cuts – before even considering tax rises.

Our personal tax system is currently highly regressive. The poorest fifth of the population pay 39.9 per cent of their income in tax, while the wealthiest fifth pays only 35.1 per cent. We need tax justice in personal taxation – which would mean higher income tax rates for the richest and cutting regressive taxes such as VAT and council tax.

Cut the real waste

While it is not necessary to cut a penny in public expenditure due to the 'deficit crisis', there are, of course, areas of public spending which could be redirected to meet social needs. In the civil and public services, we know there are massive areas of waste – such as the £1.8 billion the Government spent on private sector consultants last year. The Government could get better advice and ideas by engaging with its own staff and their trade unions.

There is also the waste of the Government having 230 separate pay bargaining units, when we could have just one national pay bargaining structure.

There are also two other large areas where government costs could be cut.

Trident

The current Trident system costs the UK around £1.5 billion every year. A private paper prepared for Nick Clegg (in 2009, when in opposition) estimated the total costs of Trident renewal amounting to between £94.7bn and £104.2bn over the lifetime of the system, estimated at 30 years. This equates to £3.3bn per year. At the time Nick Clegg (now Deputy Prime Minister) said:

> 'Given that we need to ask ourselves big questions about what our priorities are, we have arrived at the view that a like-for-like Trident replacement is not the right thing to do.'

The 2010 Liberal Democrat manifesto committed the Party to: 'Saying no to the like-for-like replacement of the Trident nuclear weapons system, which could cost £100 billion.'

PCS policy is to oppose the renewal of Trident and invest the money saved in public services, whilst safeguarding Ministry of Defence staff jobs.

War in Afghanistan

The war in Afghanistan is currently costing £2.6 billion per year. The war is both unwinnable and is making the world less safe. More important than the financial cost are the countless Afghan and British lives that are being lost in this conflict.

The PCS alternative

There is no need for cuts to public services or further privatisations

- Creating jobs will boost the economy and cut the deficit. Cutting jobs will damage the economy and increase the deficit
- We should invest in areas such as housing, renewable energy and public transport
- The UK debt is lower than other major economies
- There is a £120 billion tax gap of evaded, avoided and uncollected tax
- The UK holds £850 billion in banking assets from the bailout – this is more than the national debt
- We could free up billions by not renewing Trident
- End the use of consultants.

www.pcs.org.uk

Demythologising 'Old Labour'

Stuart Holland

Stuart Holland was directly involved in drafting Labour's Programmes from 1972 to 1983, and from 1979 to 1989 was Member of Parliament for Vauxhall.

One of the challenges which not only Ed Miliband but also others in the Parliamentary Labour Party and wider Labour movement know they need to face will be the claim from David Cameron and much of the media that the Party is reverting to 'Old Labour' and therefore doomed to fail. This article aims to help counter this by demythologising some central myths spun by the architects of 'New Labour' about Labour in the seventies and into the eighties.

It contests the claim of Gerald Kaufman that Labour's Programme 1983 was the longest suicide note in history, and contrasts this with the ironic comment from Alistair Darling, after he moved to nationalise banks in 2008, that the government's policy now was Labour's 1983 Programme. But with the difference that, while the 1983 Programme had recommended public onwership of financial institutions, this was not to salvage them and underwrite failure, rather than to ensure that savings were shifted into economic and social investments rather than financial speculation.

The article also seeks to gain context for Jim Callaghan's 'shock' statement to the 1976 Labour Conference that 'in all candour ... you can't spend your way out of recession'. For on this he was in part right. One of the limits of post-war Keynesianism was precisely that its focus on demand management had neglected that the investment horizons of big business were longer than not only annual budgets, but also of governments, and already global rather than only national, which was why Labour's Programme 1973 had made the case for Planning Agreements with such firms to seek to ensure that a demand management programme was matched by a supply response.

Jim also was frank on his learning up on this, telling me during a vote in the Commons just after the 1979 election:

'If we had been re-elected, I would have introduced Planning Agreements. I became increasingly convinced during the last government that we need them to deal with multinational companies'.[1]

This was some recognition. Planning Agreements had been stigmatised as outdated central planning, civil servants running industry and a variant on Gosplan, whereas they were based on emerging 'best practice' in continental Western Europe, and Japan. But if Jim's learning up was three years too late to help Labour in government in the 70s, Peter Mandelson took three decades to learn only half of the lesson. It was only in 2009 that the former key architect of 'business friendly' New Labour, and then Business Secretary observed, after meeting French business leaders, that:

'We have something to learn from continental practice … We are not talking about public ownership, nor are we talking about centralised planning'.

In this admission he also recognised that France was better at setting strategic goals and objectives, citing examples such as nuclear energy, high speed rail and aerospace.[2]

Yet what the by then Lord Mandelson entirely missed was that public ownership had been central to French industrial strategy in precisely these sectors of nuclear energy, high speed rail transport and aerospace. It also has been crucial to France being able to take a long-term view of investments and sustaining commitment to them. In the 1950s, French planners set the publicly owned *Electricité de France* the target of gaining four fifths of national energy through nuclear power, and achieved it without a Three Mile Island meltdown. It was through its publicly owned SCNF that it achieved its high speed TGV national rail system, now in its second generation, while Britain's privatised rail system is limping.

Without long-term finance and public ownership in sustaining Concorde, despite it never covering its development costs, France would not have retained the advanced engineering capacity in aircraft which made Airbus possible. It was not strategy alone that challenged Boeing's monopoly in civilian jet aircraft but that *Airbus Industrie* was jointly owned by governments. A cleaner, quieter and larger Concorde 2 could have been viable if Britain had not refused the offer of a joint venture in the 1960s to develop it. Britain abandoned its Blue Streak aerospace launcher and pulled out of the European launcher development organisation (ELDO). France's continued commitment to its *Diamant* launcher was the basis of its later *Ariane* and the European aerospace programme.

Also, while praising French industrial strategy, Peter Mandelson at the time was proposing to privatise the British Post Office, apparently unaware that a key to the success of planning in France has been that its publicly owned postal savings bank, the *Caisse des Depôts et Consignations*, has for decades assured a long-term supply of savings for productive investments in the private sector. He also appeared either not to know or have repressed that Labour's election manifestos in 1974, when it won two elections, had drawn centrally on both such public ownership and planning in France as a condition of value for public money in private sector whether this was through grants to them, or public purchasing from them, and that such French planning through leading firms had been a basis and legitimation of Planning Agreements in Labour's Programme 1973.

Planning Agreements

In contributinig to this, I had modelled the case for Planning Agreements on French, Italian and Belgian experience. The French case was especially compelling and almost entirely unknown in the UK until I cited it in papers I wrote for the Trade and Industry sub-committee of the Commons Expenditure Committee and the Industrial Policy Committee of the Party. Especially, the French case for planning through leading firms challenged the 'indicative planning' which had underlain Labour's 1965 National Plan.

The presumption of the National Plan, advocated by Wilson's then economic adviser Thomas Balogh, for whom I had worked for some time in the Cabinet Office, was that French planning worked through sectoral 'modernisation committees'. This had been plain to the Conservatives before 1964, who had modelled the National Economic Development Committees or NEDCs on them. But, by 1965, the French Ministry of Finance had started directly negotiated agreements with major companies – in the first instance *Contrats de Stabilité* or stability agreements, and by 1966 into *Contrats de Programme* or planning agreements.

I had learned of this shift towards planning through leading firms in January 1966 from Jean Saingeour, then Director of Planning at the French Ministry of Economy and Finance. I had walked into his office with a copy of Francois Perroux's *Techniques Quantitatives de la Planification*[3] which I had been reading. Perroux's case was that the modernisation committees were talkshops, and that what planning in a market economy needed was a workshop style agreement with *firmes motrices* or leading firms. In an oligopolistic economy, it was they who decided what was done, where, when and how. Perroux also stressed that France should compete not by lowering costs and benefits but by promoting and sustaining innovation in a Schumpeterian manner. Saingeour stressed that Perroux's approach had been very influential with the Ministry.

It had. In introducing stability agreements with leading firms, the Ministry of Economy and Finance had undertaken that they could change any prices they wished for any product, provided that their overall turnover-price ratio averaged a given rate consistent with a national target for inflation. The aim was a macro policy outcome, i.e., if big business price leaders kept to the target, it was more likely to be met.

Yet those involved in negotiating the agreements quickly realised that they had no proper knowledge of the basis on which firms were declaring costs, not least through internal and international transfer pricing. In other words, leading firms allowed their different subsidiaries to charge prices to other subsidiaries or the parent company, which inflated their cost base and under-stated real overall profits. This included research and development costs, which the Ministry had no way of evaluating at arms length, and also import costs from subsidiaries either nationally or abroad.

It was in response to this that the ministry introduced *Contrats de Programme* or planning agreements. These meant that companies had to submit information on the whole range of their costs and pricing in both their national and international operations. The Ministry also decided to use *Contrats de Programme* to make grants or public spending contracts conditional on more investment in less developed regions and greater commitment to innovation and long-term investment projects.

The scale of this operation within the Economy and Finance Ministry was striking. Half of its administrative level staff was engaged in gaining information from leading firms and negotiating Planning Agreements at a time when the British Treasury had just appointed its first economic adviser.

The outcome in France today, and the contrast with the UK, is evident. They have a public high speed TGV rail system for which they produce all the rolling stock and equipment. We do not. They still have a comprehensive French controlled industrial sector, including vehicles and trucks, tyres, electrical and mechanical engineering, chemicals, electronics and computer companies. We do not.[4] Their nuclear power generation industry works well, and has taken over what remained of Britain's. They have avoided de-industrialisation. The UK has not. Where Britain still has even a reduced civil aircraft industry, it was due to the insistence of the

French on our not backing out of Condorde, and thus preserving the base long-term for Airbus Industrie. Westland helicopters, meanwhile, has been taken over by Augusta – a subsidiary of Finmeccanica, which itself is a subsidiary of the Italian state holding company IRI, on which I had modelled the case for the National Enterprise Board, of which more below.

I used the example of the French – and parallel Belgian and Italian – planning agreements in the first paper which I submitted to the Industrial Policy Committee of the Labour Party.[5] But I had also given a paper on them, and advocated their adoption, to Harold Wilson when working for him through Thomas Balogh in the Cabinet Office.[6] I later directly advocated them to Harold in 1967 when he brought me into the Political Office in No.10. I argued that this approach – planning through leading firms – was how to re-launch The National Plan, which had collapsed with the deflationary package of July the previous year. Harold claimed to be impressed and passed the paper to Peter Shore, who had taken over from George Brown at the Department of Economic Affairs. But there was no follow through. There was no re-launch of the National Plan.

This partly influenced my decision to resign from No. 10 in 1968. I little knew at the time that I would return with Planning Agreements backed by the Labour Party National Executive Committee, every major trades union and the Party Conference in 1973. But the fact that one-to-one advocacy on the basis of precedent and detailed argument had been ineffective with a Prime Minister certainly influenced the vigour with which I pursued the Planning Agreements case thereafter through the Industrial Policy Committee of the Party.

The case for Planning Agreements as means to gain more investment and employment in the regions meanwhile had been reinforced by the second report from the Trade and Industry Sub-Committee of the Expenditure Committee, which followed their recommendation of a major British State Holding Company in *Public Money in the Private Sector.* The committee had been considering evaluation of the effectiveness of agricultural price support. But I persuaded its chair, Bill Rodgers, and he the committee, that the scope and limits of this was well known, whereas whether the government was getting value for public money in regional development grants – then running at 40% subsidy for any investment in scheduled development regions – was not.

My assessment was that companies going to the regions did so for availability of labour and would have gone there irrespective of government subsidy at such a high rate. The committee then took evidence from some 75 of the top companies in the UK. Not one of them was prepared to claim that government grants had been the decisive factor in its decision to locate new plant in the regions rather than labour availability. In this regard, we were not using public money for a public purpose but giving it needlessly, and with no return, to some of the biggest companies in the country to no effect.

The report from the Expenditure Committee confirming this[7] powerfully reinforced the case for Planning Agreements as the basis on which leading companies would be obliged to trade returns in kind – whether regional investment, or more R&D in the UK, or long-term innovative investment – in return for public grants or public purchasing or, less typically, but not ruled out, public loans.

Not least, I had documentation on both the form of Planning Agreements – their templates – as introduced in France, Italy and Belgium, and which leading companies had accepted them in these countries. I passed these to the Inflation Sub-Committee of the Industrial Policy Committee of the National Executive, in February 1973, with a cover note of half a dozen pages placing them in the context of the change within French planning has shifted from modernisation committees to direct negotiations with firms.[8] In the Belgian case I also made available summaries of actual Progress Agreements signed with leading companies such as Siemens. The Siemens agreement included commitment to a four year programme which would more than treble its investment and quadruple its employment in Belgium and open entirely new plant in the country's scheduled Development Areas. With trade union support, Siemens also committed itself to a programme for new methods of work organisation.[9]

State entrepreneurship

Such evidence legitimated the case for Planning Agreements as a complement to direct action through the state holding companies modelled on the Italian Industrial Reconstruction Institute (IRI) and the Italian State Hydrocarbons Agency (ENI).[10] Shortly after, I made exactly the same case for State shareholding in what proved to be a key paper to the Industrial Policy Committee of the Labour Party.[11] The case ran as follows:

(1) Location of modern and advanced technology companies in the regions.
(2) Channelling of government expenditure into directly productive investment as a growth promotion or counter-recession instrument.
(3) Reinforcing macro-economic trade and exchange rate policies through investment which was import-substituting or export-promoting.
(4) Countering the concentration of economic power through competitive public enterprise in both industry and finance.

(5) Offsetting short-termism by undertaking investment which private industry either was not willing to commit or unwilling to make on a scale or time horizon sufficient to meet long-term growth requirements.

(6) Promoting and reinforcing new innovation trajectories.

This case for State holdings was for making markets work in the public interest – including firms which could not gain long-term regenerative finance from stock markets (British Leyland), could not afford to innovate their own technical breakthroughs rather than license them abroad (Ferranti), or needed long-term funding to reinforce and promote what already had been considerable market success (Sinclair).

A central point about state shareholding on the IRI model was that while the main holding company would be 100% owned, the holdings in individual companies could be much less and even minority. This was not 'old style' nationalisation but the case for selective state shareholding.

It was the more compelling for the NEC at the time in view of already available figures on the marked trend to concentration in British industry. The top 100 companies had increased their share of manufacturing output from 20% in 1950 to over 40% by 1970, and their share of manufacturing employment to a third.[12] The top 30 firms accounted for a third of total UK visible export trade, the top 75 for nearly half such trade.[13]

Thus the fabric of small firms presumed by the competitive market model had given way to the dominance of two, three or four firms in any single market. In the promotion of mergers between British firms on the largely misplaced grounds of gaining economies of scale, the 1960s Labour government's Industrial Reorganisation Corporation actually had concentrated rather than countervailed such producer power.

Also, such giant firms were multinational in dual senses: either they were controlled from abroad or had invested abroad on a scale which tended to substitute for exports. Unlike Germany or Japan at the time, whose value of production from subsidiaries abroad was only two fifths of their national exports, the value of production by British firms outside Britain was more than double total UK visible export trade.

Foreign production on such a scale tended to substitute for exports, with loss of multiplier effects and growth in the domestic economy.[14] Price-making power by a handful of such multinational companies in each of the main sectors of industry was reinforced by their ability to understate exports or overstate imports in transfer pricing between domestic or foreign subsidiaries in such a way as to inflate nominal costs, reduce registered profits and avoid corporation tax.

Transfer pricing was evident to me by the early 70s from research into the electronics industry by one of my doctoral students at Sussex,[15] but also more extensively from Monopolies Commission reports. In 1974, Shirley Williams became Secretary of State for Prices and Consumer Protection. When I told her that Hoffman-La Roche was selling Librium and Valium to the NHS at £370 and £922 per kilo while an Italian company was selling them on the market for £9 and £20, she suggested that Roche halve the price, but did not follow through.[16]

When Tony Benn was Secretary of State for Energy, I alerted him to the fact that a white collar Scottish trades unionist had told me at a conference that he now understood why the prices of components from the US parent company for an oil rig being constructed on Clydeside were being inflated hand over fist every month, and that he anticipated that the company would claim the yard was unprofitable and either tell the government it had to buy and shelve the rig, or close the yard, which the company then did.

Tony knew of the problem of transfer pricing but lacked the powers to do anything about it since Harold Wilson had made Planning Agreements with multinationals 'voluntary' which, in effect, had gelded them. But this, by the mid 70s, therefore was frustrating both the Right and Left of the Labour Government, not least since transfer pricing, by inflating subsidiary component prices, reduced declared profits and tax. This was why, among other reasons, Jim Callaghan volunteered that he had become convinced that Labour government needed Planning Agreements to deal with multinational companies.

The dominance of most markets by a handful of giant multinational firms meant that the conventional micro-macro distinction in economic theory and government thinking was outdated, which had prompted me to conceptualise their power in *The Socialist Challenge*[17] as mesoeconomic, from the Greek *mesos* meaning intermediate or in between the economy of small micro firms and macro outcomes yet dominating both, which gained little resonance in mainstream economics at the time, but anticipated precisely the phenomenon of 'too big to fail', which has led to vast public subsidy of a handful of banks whose recklessness has plunged the western market economies into crisis.

The case that I made both in *The Socialist Challenge*, and to the NEC, was that indicative national planning meant little or nothing to the executives of such multinational companies other than that by sitting on National Economic Development Councils they could gain themselves a place in the honours list. In turn, their global reach already had undermined the effectiveness of the principal Keynesian demand policies, which were premised on perfect or imperfect competition on the supply side of a national economy.[18] Keynesian national fiscal and exchange rate policy was already profoundly compromised.

It was on such grounds[19] that I argued the six-point case for competitive public enterprise in my 1972 report on *European Para-Governmental Agencies* to the Expenditure Committee on Trade and Industry chaired by Bill Rodgers. The State could not countervail oligopoly power unless it itself became an entrepreneur. The cross party committee both accepted my report and then visited IRI and its affiliate companies, as well as leading private sector companies such as FIAT and Pirelli in Italy. In its own report, the Committee recommended the establishment of a British State Holding Company on the lines I had advocated.[20]

Knowing of my just published edited study of IRI in 1972, and being given a copy of it,[21] Roy Jenkins asked me whether I would draft the case for a British state holding company. He was planning a series of speeches on what the next Labour government should do, which then were published by Fontana under the title *'What Matters Now'*.[22]

I recognised Roy both as a highly progressive Home Secretary in the 1960s and as an opportunist, knew also that this was a bid for leadership of the Party, which he admitted,[23] but was not much concerned with this rather than that leading figures in the PLP should learn up on what had gone wrong in the 1960s and make the case for new dimensions to public ownership in what now were the new 'commanding heights' of the national economy, rather than the 'commanded depths' of basic industry and utilities that Labour, rightly enough, but with limited leverage on manufacturing or finance, had nationalised after the war.

Roy made plain that the first of his series of speeches would be on *The Needs of the Regions,* which had resonance then as now, and asked a question which later was to be echoed by the lesser known John Chalmers, who was the chair of the Industrial Policy Committee of the Party at the time, and which then was to hit headlines in the entirely false claim that the NEC aimed to 'nationalise' the 'top twenty five companies'. The question was how big a State Holding Company would need to be to register real gains for the regions.

I stressed that to do so it would need to be able to promote a 'broad wave'[24] of new investment by firms in the UK, otherwise there would be no net investment in entirely new plant for the regions. He asked me to analyse and spell out the sectors. I did, by an analysis of the regionally mobile or 'footloose' sectors of industry which were not location specific or capital intensive. This excluded most of the nationalised industries which either were highly capital intensive, or geologically specific, such as coal, or distribution specific, such as rail, the post, gas and electricity. I told him I was not sure he needed to cite all rather than an illustrative handful of them, but he did in the opening chapter on The Needs of the Regions in his *'What Matters Now'*.[25]

As Roy put it, the State Holding Company should be represented in:

> 'the whole wide range of the engineering and motor vehicle industries, together with hosiery and other clothing, pottery and glass, furniture, pharmaceuticals and one or two others ... [It] would have to grow steadily from the base provided by existing holdings in private industry ... But there already is a solid base, we own 49% of BP, now the largest and among the most profitable of British companies. We own Rolls Royce, we have a stake in a number of other companies. These, supplemented by a limited amount of selected nationalization, should provide a good base from which to diversify into the labour-using industries which the regions require.'[26]

As for finance to embark on what Roy called the State Holding Company's 'extensive programme of acquisition and diversification', this should come partly from its own profits, partly from Government grants, and partly from the capital market'.[27] Roy's case, as thus published, was more radical in scope – 'the whole wide range of engineering' and 'its extensive programme of acquisition and diversification', plus only a management constraint on its rate of growth – than the NEC Green Paper on The National Enterprise Board, which limited its build up over time to shareholdings in from twenty to twenty five companies.[28] It required short-term amnesia, or failure to read it first, for Jenkins to condemn the NEC Green Paper as 'outdated nationalisation dogma' and then seek to contrast it with his case for state shareholdings in his *What Matters Now*.

So what now?

So what lessons can be learned from this now by Labour with a new leadership? There is only scope here to draw some of them, which relate to countering myths in order to better confront current realities.

The first is that the case of Labour's Programmes from 1973 through to and including the 1983 Programme was not for 'outdated nationalisation' or civil servants running industry or a variant on Gosplan but for making markets work in the public interest and gaining accountability for public money in the private sector.

The second is that the case first was endorsed by the Right of the Party, in the case of Bill Rodgers and Roy Jenkins, who knew it well since Bill

Rodgers had chaired the Expenditure Committee of the Commons, which had gained cross party support, and Roy Jenkins had endorsed it in his 1972 *What Matters Now,* before they both reneged on it when it was adopted by the NEC.

The third is that this was well informed by advanced industrial strategy in economies such as France and Italy where success had been based on the combination of public ownership and planning at the level of leading firms.

The fourth is that this was not 'Old Labour' looking back but already a 'New' Labour case, based on recognising trends in globalisation and the need to countervail them to avoid de-industrialisation and the loss of effective taxation through transfer pricing and other techniques adopted by multinational capital.

The fifth is the need to recognise that de-industrialisation has occurred and that an industrial strategy now needs to be regional, through the regional development agencies, which were part of Labour's 1973 Programme, were introduced in the case of the Scottish, Welsh and Northern Ireland Development Agencies and, from 1997, in England.

The sixth is that Labour should not only salvage banks but also manage them in the public interest, which will become more relevant to what is needed if the cuts in deficits in the UK and Europe result in a double-dip recession.

There are others. One is recovering the principle of mutual societies as a means of safeguarding personal savings and investments, which they were before the appropriately named 1986 'Big Bang' of bank liberalisation began the process by which mutuals then were allowed to speculate with such savings.

Another is making more use of European finance through the European Investment Bank which, since 1997, has been able to fund investments in health, education, urban regeneration, the environment and green technology with the advantage also that such finance need not count on the public sector borrowing requirement.

All of which can contribute to the claim of John Smith that markets should serve people and not people serve markets.

Notes

1 He prefaced this by allowing that I might not believe him. But I did, since there was an implicit logic in any national government needing to gain leverage on big business for the use of public money in the private sector. Jim also asked whether I would prepare material concerning the activities of multinationals for a speech he was to give shortly on the subject, which I duly did.

2 Hollinger, P. (2009). Mandelson praise for French strategy. *Financial Times*. March 15th.

3 Francois Perroux, *Les Techniques Quantitatives de la Planification,* Presses Universitaires de France, 1965.

4 Even our long standing major companies such as GEC in electrical and mechanical engineering and ICI in chemicals have been stripped down or hollowed out.

5 The Italian version of Planning Agreements or Programmazione Contrattata, were mainly concerned with gaining regional investment by private companies in Southern Italy.

6 Stuart Holland, *French Incomes and Prices Policy*, Cabinet Office, 2 December 1966.

7 Second Report from the Expenditure Committee, Session 1973-4, *Regional Development Incentives,* HMSO December 1973.

8 Stuart Holland, *Inflation and Price Control: Note on French Programme Contracts*, Labour Party Working Group on Inflation, RD 605, February 1973.

9 Employment was to increase from 1,100 to 4,100 jobs in electronics and computers, telecommunications and medical equipment. Contrat de Progrès Entre l'État Belge et S.A. Siemens, ST. no. 265/ 8.5. 1970.

10 Memorandum on European Para-Governmental Agencies, in *Sixth Report from the Expenditure Committee: Public Money in the Private Sector*, vol III, pp. 740-753.

11 Stuart Holland, *Planning and Policy Coordination*, Paper to the Industrial Policy Committee of the Labour Party, RD 315, March 1972.

12 See further *The Annual Census of Production* and S.J. Prais, *The Evolution of Giant Firms in Britain*, Cambridge University Press, 1976. Professor Prais' had kindly made the key figures of his study available to me for use before publication.

13 See further *The Department of Trade's Annual Overseas Transactions Enquiry*, HMSO. The top 75 firms reached the 50% share of visible export trade in 1975.

14 Bertil Ohlin gained the Nobel Prize for Economics in the work in which he pointed this out, although point thereafter was lost to most theorists of international trade. Cf. Bertil Ohlin, *Interregional and Interrnational Trade*, Harvard University press, 1933 and revised edition 1967.

15 Edmond Scribberas, *Multinational Electronics Companies and National Economic Policies*, JAI Press, Greenwich, Connecticut, 1977.

16 Hoffman-La Roche was quick to point out that the Italian company had disregarded its patents, and claim that the price difference reflected its R&D costs. But Shirley Williams appears to have made no effort to ask for a revelation of such costs, or the transfer price.

17 Stuart Holland, *The Socialist Challenge,* Quartet Books, London, 1975.

18 Perfect competition assumed that firms were price takers from sovereign consumers rather than price makers. Imperfect competition simply argued that

firms priced on a cost plus profit basis, rather than maximised profits and minimized tax by transfer pricing between their subsidiaries.

19 See *inter alia* my contribution to Wayland Kennet, Larry Whitty and Stuart Holland, *Sovereignty and Multinational Companies,* Fabian Tract 409, July 1971, for many of whose insights I was much indebtted then as now to Robin Murray, at the time with the London Business School, later at the Institute of Development Studies at Sussex and later head of the employment committee of the Greater London Council.

20 Memorandum on the Visit of the Trade and Industry Sub-Committee to Italy, April 1972, in *Sixth Report from the Expenditure Committee: Public Money in the Private Sector*, vol III, pp. 753-773.

21 Stuart Holland (Ed) *The State as Entrepreneur: the IRI State Shareholding Formula*, Weidenfeld and Nicolson, 1972.

22 Roy Jenkins, *What Matters Now*, Fontana Paperback, Collins/Fontana, London, 1972.

23 At a lunch with me and Eric Roll, who had been the permanent secretary to George Brown at the Department of Economic Affairs.

24 This 'broad wave' approach had been advocated by Ragnar Nurkse and Paul Rosenstein-Rodan. Their case, however, had been for broad ranging infrastructure in countries which lacked it, rather than through companies.

25 Roy Jenkins (1972), *What Matters Now*, Fontana Paperback, Collins/Fontana, London, op cit.

26 Roy Jenkins, ibid. p. 35ff. 'Hosiery and other clothing' were his idea, not mine. But they took his recommendations that a State Holding Company should be represented into more than the twenty to twenty five sectors which the next year was to be advocated by the National Executive of the Party.

27 Roy Jenkins, ibid. pp. 35-36.

28 The Labour Party, The National Enterprise Board, Opposition Green Paper, London, April1973.

Failing Intelligence

Brian Jones

Dr Jones was head of the UK Defence Intelligence Staff's nuclear, biological and chemical weapons section in the build up to the invasion and occupation of Iraq. This article is based on a lecture he gave at the Royal United Services Institute in September 2010 to launch his book, Failing Intelligence: The true story of how we were fooled into going to war in Iraq (£9.99 BiteBack).

In the year or so following my retirement in early 2003, I gave evidence on intelligence and weapons of mass destruction to two of the four inquiries on Iraq – namely Hutton and Butler. I was less than completely satisfied with what emerged from these, and indeed the other two inquiries, by the Foreign Affairs Committee and the Intelligence and Security Committee, so, through 2004, I wrote a number of articles and gave a number of interviews trying to clarify what I believed had happened and what had been missed.

Going in to 2005, I was becoming increasingly frustrated with what I saw as the failure of my attempts to explain, in the space or time available, the whole complex of issues that lay behind the mistake that had been made on Iraq and WMD. These issues include:

- the weird, sometimes wonderful, and often frustrating world of intelligence
- the confusing practices and processes of the Whitehall machine and the governance that emanates from it, and
- the technically complicated subjects of nuclear, chemical and biological agents and weapons which are quite different one from another in terms of their utility, potential and control.

It was then I decided it would take a book to do all these things properly, and that is where most of my energies on this subject went to after that. I have divided my book into four parts:

I Context
II Deception
III Cover-up, and
IV Conclusion

I use the Context to try and explain the background to some of the issues I mentioned a moment ago, using the experience of my own introduction to them to aid my description. Then I spend some time in the period 1990-2000, discussing the intelligence background to the first Gulf War and the difficulty of establishing that Iraq had disarmed. I also raise the issue of whether it was ever the intention of the US to let Saddam off the hook by allowing that he had disarmed. In other words, would that eventuality ever have been in line with the US Liberation Act that President Clinton signed in 1998 and some believe had been unofficial US policy since the administration of George Bush Senior, in the early 1990s.

The impact of 9/11 in 2001 is an obvious element in the overall context since it ignited 'the war on terror', Afghanistan and 'enabled' the US invasion of Iraq in 2003. But I also say a little about the impact of the 'anthrax letters' that followed closely on 9/11, and had a great effect on Washington. Some of the witnesses to the Chilcot inquiry have drawn attention to the importance of this incident.

In 'Deception' I look at the events of 2002 starting with the State of the Union address in January, the flurry of papers that followed it in Whitehall before the Crawford summit in April, and finishing with the secret Downing Street meeting of 23 July.

I then discuss the events surrounding the generation of the September 2002 dossier which, depending on who you listen to, was or was not making a case for war. I will return to one aspect of this.

It was in the period between the dossier and the war that I retired, in January 2003. There were several important developments in that period – a fascinating meeting I attended in the Cabinet Office, Bush's UN speech followed by Resolution 1441, Alistair Campbell's dodgy dossier, Colin Powell's speech at the UN, and important resignations from the government on the eve of war.

It is at this point that I discuss how I felt at the time about our participation in the war. There was no justification in terms of Iraq's immediate WMD capabilities because we simply could not be sure they were there. But if you set that aside, I was prepared to admit there could be a 'big picture' case for it – not so much based on Iraq's future WMD capabilities, which now seems to be a favourite fall-back position for Mr Blair and his former staff at No. 10, but for a number of other reasons which I discuss in the book.

I suspect those concerned, both politicians and officials, knew they were taking a risk when they made Iraq's 'current' possession of WMD the overwhelming justification for war. I believe the decisions were taken with the best of intentions by all concerned, and I am not advocating a witch-hunt or the attribution of blame.

But it has been the failure of those involved to acknowledge, in any substantial way, that the risk they took failed, which prompted me to devote a major part of my book to the 'Cover-up' of what happened. Not least because none of the four inquiries completed so far has looked at this aspect, and I see little evidence that this is something the Chilcot Inquiry has pursued. Why is it important?

Because it has obstructed the identification of some important lessons about how things went so horribly wrong, and was a factor in Whitehall choosing to ignore some others that were identified, mainly by the Butler review. It meant that the line the government wanted to draw under the matter could not be drawn, and has still to be drawn. It created the impression of a nation complicit in and supportive of a war that lacked legitimacy, even after it became clear that the WMD justification was without foundation. And it undermined confidence in our politics and governance even before the Expenses Crisis dealt it yet another fearsome blow.

And I conclude my book by discussing the impact I believe all of this is likely to have had on three issues that remain high profile: nuclear, biological and chemical weapons proliferation and arms control, terrorism, and intelligence.

Turning now to the issue I want to focus on in a little more detail. If it was to get the support that would be needed for probable military operations, the government had to convince the public and Parliament of an imminent threat from Iraq's WMD that was significant enough for British troops to die for. A fundamental requirement for this, of course, was that Iraq had to have significant quantities of chemical or biological weapons to pose such a threat. Intelligence did not allow such an assessment until at least the end of August 2002 when up popped a number of intelligence reports that *some* thought seemed to fit the bill. These arrived in the middle of the assessment process of a Joint Intelligence Committee paper, which was due for approval on 4 September. As it considered the draft assessment, the JIC was told of the important new intelligence that had only recently arrived and the Assessments Staff were told to include some of this before the report was issued. The report was finally issued a few days later, on 9 September.

In fact, the new intelligence, as far as I read the situation, was so weak that the Assessments Staff struggled to use it. In the end they incorporated just one sentence and they buried it deep in the text. It was this:

> 'Intelligence also indicates that biological and chemical munitions could be with military units and ready for firing within 20-45 minutes.'
>
> *JIC (02) 202, Iraqi use of Chemical Biological Weapons –*
> *Possible Scenarios – 9ᵗʰ September 2002*

We can discuss why this is such a weak statement, but if it had been true it would not only have shown that Iraq had both chemical and biological munitions, but also that it had them in sufficient quantities for the deployment implied by that statement. We had no other credible evidence that this was the case.

But the statement in the JIC assessment was not strong enough for the Prime Minister's dossier, which was being hurriedly drafted at the same time. The drafters now tried to harden it up for the dossier but the analysts said no, and there was deadlock. Then, suddenly, obviously too late for the JIC paper on 9th September, up popped something else. No. 10 was told about it on 12th September, although on the basis of his evidence to Chilcot, Tony Blair doesn't seem to recall this piece of intelligence. Conveniently, the intelligence says, and we now know it says this much, that production of agent or weapons or both had indeed taken place. Unfortunately, it was from a new source said to be on trial and, as far as I can gather, there was never any collateral around for it except that which was given by each of these reports, the 45 Minute report and this report, which were both from shaky sources. That was the only, relatively poor collateral that seemed to me to exist.

I've call this second report 'Report X' – X for the unknown, because only a very few people knew what was in that report, and I don't think many more people know what was in it to this day. It was not shown to the intelligence analysts at the time – it was said to be too sensitive – but it was enough to break the deadlock.

And this is what happened really. Bearing in mind the weak statement in the JIC paper quoted above, the Joint Intelligence Committee said in its Executive Summary of the dossier

'We judge that some of these weapons are deployable within 45 minutes of an order to use them.'

The Prime Minister then said in his Foreword

'I am in no doubt that the threat is serious and current … And the document discloses that his [Saddam's] military planning allows for some of the WMD to be ready within 45 minutes of an order to use them.'

Thus the analysts were overruled. The Joint Intelligence Committee could sign off on the dossier, and did not argue, as far as anyone has admitted, with the Prime Minister's assertion that it left no doubt that Iraq had weapons of mass destruction.

Despite not being mentioned in the dossier or, I think, in any JIC assessment, in the true tradition of the mysterious world of intelligence, it's invisible presence, the invisible presence of Report X, was the single most important element in the government's case for war. We know a remarkable amount about the 45 minute intelligence report, but clearly it was not strong enough to stand alone. It needed to be stood up by Report X. But seven years and four inquiries on, we still know very little about what was actually in Report X. When the experts finally saw it – probably shortly after the war – I understand they dismissed it quite quickly.

The Foreign Affairs Committee Inquiry did not know about this report at all when they conducted their inquiry, and it was kept out of Hutton until I mentioned it in my evidence, which was well into the Inquiry, and after quite a lot of government witnesses had given evidence where it really would have been very much more convenient to talk about it. Hutton, I believe, was never shown the actual report. In fact, the report had been withdrawn even before Hutton started seeing witnesses – and certainly, I did not know that, and I don't think Hutton knew that it had been withdrawn either. The withdrawal was first revealed by the Panorama team, and confirmed within days by the Butler report, six months after Hutton reported.

Reading between the lines of its report, it appears to me, that attempts were made to keep Report X away from the Intelligence and Security Committee, but they did eventually get to see it, and knew it had been withdrawn. But the ISC did not mention either its withdrawal or any uncertainty about its sourcing in its report. The ISC said this of Report X:

> 'We were told that there was further intelligence of a nature so sensitive that it was only released on a very restricted basis. We have seen that intelligence and understand the basis on which CDI and the JIC took the view they did.'

Now that sounded to me, at the time, like an endorsement of Report X, and indeed some had suggested it was, both in the House and in evidence to the inquiries. But when I discussed it with a member of the ISC a few months later, I was told that the statement was intended to be obviously Delphic in nature and, whilst the Committee did not endorse the view, it could understand how others might.

The Butler review, of course, did see Report X. The Butler report describes Report X as being from 'a new source on trial' and about 'Iraqi production of chemical and biological agents' which 'had been accelerated by the Iraqi regime, including through the building of further facilities throughout Iraq'.

Butler acknowledges that Report X provided significant assurance to those drafting the dossier that agent was actively being produced, but does not go so far as to explain, very clearly at least, the context of it breaking the deadlock associated with the approval of the dossier by the Defence Intelligence Staff as a body. The withdrawal of Report X in July 2003 is described as being about its sourcing or the lack of reliability of its sourcing.

However, nothing is said, as far as I can see, about the quality of the intelligence contained in the report:
– How much sense did it make?
– How specific was it?
– Did it identify the agents involved?
– Did the source say anything about how they were produced? Or how much was produced?
– Where they were produced and stored?
– Was there significant collateral for what was said?
– Was collateral sought and found between September 2002, when it appeared, and March 2003 when the war began?

We don't know the answers to these questions.

Of the reporting up to the time of the Joint Intelligence Committee's paper of 9 September, Butler commented that 'we were struck by the relative thinness of the intelligence base supporting the greater firmness of the JIC's judgements on Iraqi production and possession of chemical and biological weapons'.

Butler expressed no view on whether it believed Report X added significant depth to that intelligence base. I suspect it did not. And I think it is about time that Parliament and the public were told more about that, and about the retrospective analysis that surely must have been done on that report given its importance. Because I believe that will tell us something about the qualities of the decision made by those who obviously decided it was convincing.

The whole subject of Report X, to my mind, raises important issues about how our intelligence machine worked at that time. Butler did identify a lot of the problems, but there were a few that it did not identify. The implementation of the Butler recommendations has left a few important ones out, and I don't think the potential major flaws in the system have been resolved. In the book I identify what I believe these flaws are. I discuss them, and provide suggestions for their resolution in some detail.

Perhaps it is time for me to give you some bottom lines on the consequences of the Iraq war that may prove to have significance greater than the war itself.

It is my view that the Iraq war has set back the wider cause of nuclear, biological, chemical arms control and non-proliferation.

It, and other aspects of the 'war on terror', may arguably have pushed some elements of the threat from international terrorism to the right, but I respect the judgements of the former head of MI5, Baroness Manningham-Buller, as she gave them to the Iraq Inquiry. In particular, the war appears to have unleashed something in the UK that might otherwise have been kept in check and, as the recent report of the Royal United Services Institute apparently suggests, there maybe unforeseen consequences in train yet.

Finally, I think British intelligence has yet to recover from the credibility it lost over Iraq. If our Foreign and Defence policy outlook, as a result of the review in progress at the moment, is not to change, then I think this is of great importance. I suggest that the intelligence machine should be subjected to a thorough, independent review and that, perhaps, a major top-end organisational change should be considered.

www.bitebackpublishing.com

Scared of the facts

Hans von Sponeck

Hans von Sponeck worked for the United Nations Development Programme for 32 years. In 1998, he was appointed UN Humanitarian Co-ordinator for Iraq. He resigned in March 2000 in protest at the sanctions on Iraq which were causing the Iraqi people great suffering. Here, in an open letter, he responds to some of the claims made in Tony Blair's book, A Journey.

Dear Mr Blair,
You do not know me. Why should you? Or maybe you should have known me and the many other UN officials who struggled in Iraq when you prepared your Iraq policy. Reading the Iraq details of your 'journey', as told in your memoir, has confirmed my fears. You tell a story of a leader, but not of a statesman. You could have, at least belatedly, set the record straight. Instead you repeat all the arguments we have heard before, such as why sanctions had to be the way they were; why the fear of Saddam Hussein outweighed the fear of crossing the line between concern for people and power politics; why Iraq ended up as a human garbage can. You preferred to latch on to Bill Clinton's 1998 Iraq Liberation Act and George W Bush's determination to implement it.

You present yourself as the man who tried to use the UN road. I am not sure. Is it really wrong to say that, if you had this intention, it was for purely tactical reasons and not because you wanted to protect the role of the UN to decide when military action was justified? The list of those who disagreed with you and your Government's handling of 13 years of sanctions and the invasion and occupation of Iraq is long, very long. It includes Unicef and other UN agencies, Care, Caritas, International Physicians for the Prevention of Nuclear War, the then UN Secretary General, Kofi Annan, and Nelson Mandela. Do not forget, either, the hundreds of thousands of people who marched in protest in Britain and across the world, among them Cambridge Against Sanctions on Iraq (CASI) and the UK Stop the War Coalition.

You suggest that you and your supporters – the 'people of good will', as you call them

– are the owners of the facts. Your disparaging observations about Clare Short, a woman with courage who resigned as International Development Secretary in 2003, make it clear you have her on a different list. You appeal to those who do not agree to pause and reflect. I ask you to do the same. Those of us who lived in Iraq experienced the grief and misery that your policies caused. UN officials on the ground were not 'taken in' by a dictator's regime. We were 'taken in' by the challenge to tackle human suffering, created by the gravely faulty policies of two governments – yours and that of the United States – and by the gutlessness of those in the Middle East, Europe and elsewhere who could have made a difference but chose otherwise. The facts are on our side, not on yours.

Here are some of those facts. Had Hans Blix, the then UN Chief Weapons Inspector, been given the additional three months he requested, your plans could have been thwarted. You and George W Bush feared this. If you had respected international law, you would not, following Operation Desert Fox in December 1998, have allowed your forces to launch attacks from two no-fly zones. Allegedly carried out to protect Iraqi Kurds in the north and Iraqi Shias in the south, these air strikes killed civilians and destroyed non-military installations.

I know that the reports we prepared in Baghdad to show the damage wreaked by these air strikes caused much anger in Whitehall. A conversation I had on the sidelines of the Labour Party conference in 2004 with your former Foreign Secretary, Robin Cook, confirmed that, even in your cabinet, there had been grave doubts about your approach. UN Resolution 688 was passed in 1991 to authorise the UN Secretary General – no one else – to safeguard the rights of people and to help in meeting their humanitarian needs. It did not authorise the no-fly zones. In fact, the British government, in voting for Resolution 688, accepted the obligation to respect Iraq's sovereignty and territorial integrity.

I was a daily witness to what you and two US administrations had concocted for Iraq: a harsh and uncompromising sanctions regime punishing the wrong people. Your officials must have told you that your policies translated into a meagre 51 US cents to finance a person's daily existence in Iraq. You acknowledge that 60 per cent of Iraqis were totally dependent on the goods that were allowed into their country under sanctions, but you make no reference in your book to how the UK and US governments blocked and delayed huge amounts of supplies that were needed for survival. In mid-2002, more than $5bn worth of supplies were blocked from entering the country. No other country on the Iraq sanctions committee of the UN Security Council supported you in this. The UN files are full of such evidence. I saw the education system, once a pride of Iraq, totally collapse. And conditions in the health sector were equally desperate. In 1999, the entire country had only one fully functioning X-ray machine. Diseases that had been all but forgotten in the country re-emerged.

You refuse to acknowledge that you and your policies had anything to do with this humanitarian crisis. You even argue that the death rate of children under five in Iraq, then among the highest in the world, was entirely due to the Iraqi government. I beg you to read Unicef's reports on this subject and what Carol Bellamy, Unicef's American executive director at the time, had to say to the Security Council. None of the UN officials involved in dealing with the crisis will subscribe to your view that Iraq 'was free to buy as much food and medicines' as the government would allow. I wish that had been the case. During the Chilcot inquiry in July this year, a respected diplomat who represented the UK on the Security Council sanctions committee while I was in Baghdad observed:

> 'UK officials and ministers were well aware of the negative effects of sanctions, but preferred to blame them on the Saddam regime's failure to implement the oil-for-food programme.'

No one in his right mind would defend the human rights record of Saddam Hussein. Your critical words in this respect are justified. But you offer only that part of this gruesome story. You quote damning statements about Saddam Hussein made by Max van der Stoel, the former Dutch Foreign Minister who was UN special rapporteur on human rights in Iraq during the time I served in Baghdad. You conveniently omitted three pertinent facts: van der Stoel had not been in Iraq since 1991 and had to rely on second-hand information; his UN mandate was limited to assessing the human rights record of the Iraqi government and therefore excluded violations due to other reasons such as economic sanctions; and his successor, Andreas Mavrommatis, formerly Foreign Secretary in Cyprus, quickly recognised the biased UN mandate and broadened the scope of his review to include sanctions as a major human rights issue. This was a very important correction.

Brazil's Foreign Minister, Celso Amorim, who in the years of sanctions on Iraq was his country's permanent representative to the UN, is not mentioned in your book. Is that because he was one of the diplomats who climbed over the wall of disinformation and sought the truth about the deplorable human conditions in Iraq in the late 1990s? Amorim used the opportunity of his Presidency of the UN Security Council to call for a review of the humanitarian situation. His conclusion was unambiguous.

'Even if not all the suffering in Iraq can be imputed to external factors, especially sanctions, the Iraqi people would not be undergoing such deprivations in the absence of the prolonged measures imposed by the Security Council and the effects of war.'

Malaysia's ambassador to the UN, Hasmy Agam, starkly remarked:

'How ironic it is that the same policy that is supposed to disarm Iraq of its weapons of mass destruction has itself become a weapon of mass destruction.'

The Secretary General, too, made very critical observations on the humanitarian situation in Iraq. When I raised my own concerns in a newspaper article, your minister Peter Hain repeated what the world had become accustomed to hearing from London and Washington: it is all of Saddam's making. Hain was a loyal ally of yours. He and others in your administration wrote me off as subjective, straying off my mandate, not up to the task, or, in the words of the US State Department's spokesman at the time, James Rubin: 'This man in Baghdad is paid to work, not to speak!'

My predecessor in Baghdad, Denis Halliday, and I were repeatedly barred from testifying to the Security Council. On one occasion, the US and UK governments, in a joint letter to the Secretary General, insisted that we did not have enough experience with sanctions and therefore could not contribute much to the debate. You were scared of the facts.

We live in serious times, which you helped bring about. The international security architecture is severely weakened, the UN Security Council fails to solve crises peacefully, and there are immense double standards in the debate on the direction our world is travelling in. A former British prime minister – 'a big player, a world leader and not just a national leader', as you describe yourself in your book – should find little time to promote his 'journey' on a US talk show. You decided differently. I watched this show, and a show it was. You clearly felt uncomfortable. Everything you and your brother-in-arms, Bush, had planned for Iraq has fallen apart, the sole exception being the removal of Saddam Hussein. You chose to point to Iran as the new danger.

Whether you like it or not, the legacy of your Iraq journey, made with your self-made global positioning system, includes your sacrifice of the UN and negotiations on the altar of a self-serving alliance with the Bush administration. You admit in your book that 'a few mistakes were made here and there'. One line reads: 'The intelligence was wrong and we should have, and I have, apologised for it.' A major pillar of your case for invading Iraq is treated almost like a footnote. Your refusal to face the facts fully is the reason why 'people of good will' remain so distressed and continue to demand accountability.

Afghanistan
Nail the myth

Caroline Lucas MP

The Green Party MP for Brighton Pavilion intervened in the Parliamentary debate on Afghanistan, which took place on 9 September 2010. These excerpts are taken from what she said.

It's an important tradition of this House that the names of those brave troops who have been killed in Afghanistan are read out at the beginning of each week's Prime Minister's Questions. Yesterday, that roll call seemed to go on forever. And after it, the Deputy Prime Minister said

> 'Each of those men was an heroic, selfless individual who has given his life for the safety of us and the British people.'

Each of those men was heroic and selfless – our troops are doing an extraordinary job with great courage – but I think we need to nail the myth that their presence in Afghanistan is making the British people safer. We are constantly told that our troops are fighting in that country to keep us safe in this one. But we know the terror plots against Britain weren't hatched in Afghanistan, but in Pakistan and Britain itself. On that logic, we should be sending tanks into Dewsbury.

The Afghan war was put to the British people on a simple premise – that it was an act of self-defence in response to 9/11. The objective was supposed to be to capture and kill Osama Bin Laden and prevent al Qaeda using Afghanistan as a base from which to launch further attacks. But now that rationale seems a distant memory. Al Qaeda has been effectively dispersed around the world, particularly over the border into Pakistan. So now the objective is something else – to defeat the Taliban, which once hosted Bin Laden, and to reshape Afghanistan into a functioning society which can never again give shelter to al Qaeda. Yet stepping up this war seems to be terribly misguided. If al Qaeda remains the ultimate enemy rather than the Taliban, then it makes no sense to spill so much blood in Afghanistan.

Or we are told that troops are there to bring human rights to Afghanistan. But while there was some improvement in human rights between 2001 and 2005, they are again drastically deteriorating. For many Afghans, especially those outside Kabul, improvements were anyway slight or non-existent. Vicious warlords in rural areas can be just as bent on enforcing sharia law as the Taliban.

According to Malalai Joya, the outspoken woman MP who was expelled from parliament, the government of Hamid Karzai is 'full of warlords and extremists who are brothers in creed of the Taliban', notably the judiciary, which is 'dominated by fundamentalists'. This is the President whose authority our troops are dying to defend. A President who passes into law the so-called 'marital rape' law, which gives a husband the right to withdraw basic maintenance for his wife if she refuses to obey his sexual demands.

Amnesia

When it comes to Afghanistan, it seems that we are struck by a particular kind of amnesia. There is so much we have forgotten. As Dan Plesch of the Centre for International Studies and Diplomacy has said, there is no sense that we sought to crush and dominate that country throughout the 19th and 20th centuries. We appear to have no memory of that – but the Afghans do.

There is no sense, either, that the sentiment expressed by advocates of war time and time again – that to pull out now would be a betrayal of those who have given their lives so far – is the same sentiment expressed the last time the United States and its allies feared they were about to get sucked into a foreign quagmire. Advocates of escalation in Vietnam used to say that, too: we have to send more men to die, otherwise those already dead will have died in vain.

Or we might remember the last time a mighty superpower tried to subdue Afghanistan. The Soviet Union invaded in 1979, and within a few years their soldiers were losing their limbs or lives to landmines – the improvised explosive devices of their day – and there were the same kinds of angry complaints about a shortage of helicopters. As the journalist Jonathan Freedland has said, whatever other reactions we should have to the fate of the US-led coalition in Afghanistan – horror, grief, despair – surprise should not be one of them.

It is not unpatriotic to seek to recognise that there is no military solution to the crisis in Afghanistan, and to bring our troops safely home. Almost everyone agrees that there will have to be a negotiated regional settlement sooner or later. Let's make it sooner, and stop the bloodshed now.

Human Cost

This amnesia has an enormous human cost. The evidence of escalating violence and increasing insecurity in Afghanistan is reinforced by the WikiLeaks circulation back in July of huge amounts of official communications and reports about the US war on the ground. The leaked war logs also reveal that coalition forces have tried to cover up the fact that they have killed hundreds of civilians in unreported incidents. As they increasingly use deadly Reaper drones to hunt and kill Taliban targets under remote control from a base in Nevada, civilian deaths or collateral damage rise still further.

As of August 2010, over 330 British forces personnel or Ministry of Defence civilians had died while serving in Afghanistan, with several thousand more injured. Over 1000 US troops have died. And what of the Afghan casualties?

Of course, no official count is kept, but the estimate is at many thousands. Civilian casualties from the fighting have risen every year since 2001 but figures are very hard to arrive at. The International Security Assistance Force's own confidential report of August 2009 concedes that its military strategy is causing 'unnecessary collateral damage'. Leaders publicly say that their attacks are proportionate. Yet US Lt Col David Kilcullen has said that US aerial attacks on the Afghan-Pakistan border have killed 14 al Qaeda leaders at the expense of 700 civilian lives.

Alongside US and British military in Afghanistan is a 'shadow army' of private military and security companies, operating largely outside legal or democratic control. As a recent article in *Le Monde Diplomatique* asked, in characteristic diplomatic language, 'How can efforts to put down an insurgency be effective or credible when the countries contributing to the intervention force, and representing the UN, use mercenaries whose motivation is not necessarily the restoration of peace?' Or, as one British contractor is quoted as saying, rather more bluntly, in a War on Want briefing on this subject, for his firm, the more the security situation deteriorated, the better it is for business.

Extraordinary rendition – worse than Guantanamo

We also know that Afghanistan is a key link in the network of secret prisons used by the US for unlawful detention and torture, and there are plenty of signs that Britain is intimately involved. The best known of the

Afghan 'secret' prisons is within Bagram airbase. As of late 2009, the Pentagon reported 645 prisoners being held at Bagram, supposedly terrorist suspects. The Obama administration has continued to block granting legal rights to the detainees – so none has a right to a lawyer, and no civilian lawyer, or journalist, has ever been there.

US lawyer Tina Foster, who is arguing several cases on behalf of detainees at Bagram, says that, from the beginning, 'Bagram was worse than Guantanamo', and 'has always been a torture chamber'. And rather than closing Bagram, the Obama administration is expanding it to hold five times as many prisoners as Guantanamo.

Afghan Development

All of this might not be quite as horrific if the lives of ordinary Afghans were significantly improving, and the country developing. But although, on some indicators, there has been some improvement – on access to education, for example – overall the situation is bleak. Indeed, by some indicators, Afghans are getting poorer – child malnutrition, for example, has risen in some areas, an effect of the chronic hunger that now affects over 7 million people.

Meanwhile:

● 1 in 5 children dies before the age of 5, the highest infant mortality rate in the world;
● A shocking 1 in 8 Afghan women die from causes related to pregnancy and childbirth;
● Life expectancy is just 44.

The United States has spent 20 times as much on military operations than on development in Afghanistan, while Britain has spent 10 times as much. Yet the UN Security Council notes that 25 as many Afghans die every year from under-nutrition and poverty as from violence.

This is an unwinnable war that is costing us over £7 million a day. If George Osborne is looking at places to cut spending, he should start right here, and bring the troops home. But the financial cost to Afghanistan is huge as well. The Afghan government spends a massive 30% of its budget on the security sector. In 2008, it was spending seven times more than the world average on the military, and more than twice as much as most other countries undergoing war.

I want to conclude by noting that Britain is in many respects a bigger recruiting sergeant for the Taliban than al Qaeda ever was. ISAF's Director of Intelligence provided a briefing, in December 2009, that outlined information given by militants to the International Security Assistance

Force. It states they view al Qaeda as a 'handicap', and that this view is 'increasingly prevalent'.

Instead, the insurgents were motivated by the government being seen as corrupt and ineffective, by crime and corruption being pervasive among the security forces, and because promised infrastructure projects were ineffective.

Increasing civilian deaths is also likely to be another driver for villagers joining the insurgents, together with a lack of other viable ways of making any money. In that respect, when the government argues that leaving Afghanistan now would provide a boost for al Qaeda, in fact the opposite is true.

The longer the occupation continues, the more jihadists around the world will be likely to be inspired to target Britain, and the more Afghan villagers are likely to side with the insurgents. That's why I believe that British and other NATO troops must halt their offensive military activities and announce a timetable for withdrawal as soon as possible. We should be engaging in talks to secure a regional solution to the war now.

The sun in the sky

Matt Waldman scrutinises Pakistan's role in Afghanistan.

Many accounts of the Afghan conflict misapprehend the nature of the relationship between Pakistan's security services and the insurgency. The relationship, in fact, goes far beyond contact and coexistence, with some assistance provided by elements within, or linked to, Pakistan's intelligence service (ISI) or military.

Although the Taliban has a strong endogenous impetus, according to Taliban commanders the ISI orchestrates, sustains and strongly influences the movement. They say it gives sanctuary to both Taliban and Haqqani groups, and provides huge support in terms of training, funding, munitions, and supplies. In their words, this is 'as clear as the sun in the sky'.

Directly or indirectly the ISI appears to exert significant influence on the strategic decision making and field operations of the Taliban; and has even greater sway over Haqqani insurgents. According to both Taliban and Haqqani commanders, it controls the most violent insurgent units, some of which appear to be based in Pakistan. Insurgent commanders confirmed that the ISI are even represented, as participants or observers, on the Taliban supreme leadership council, known as the Quetta Shura, and the Haqqani command council. Indeed, the agency appears to have circumscribed the Taliban's strategic autonomy, precluding steps towards talks with the Afghan government through recent arrests.

President Zardari himself has apparently assured captive, senior Taliban leaders that they are 'our people' and have his backing. He has also apparently authorised their release from prison. The ISI even arrested and then released two Taliban leaders, Qayyum Zakir, the movement's new military commander, and Mullah Abdul Raouf Khadem, reportedly now head of the Quetta Shura, who are among the three or four highest ranking in the movement below Mullah Omar.

Pakistan's apparent involvement in a double-game of this scale could have major geopolitical implications and could even provoke US counter-measures. However, the powerful role of the ISI, and parts of the Pakistani military, suggests that progress against the Afghan insurgency, or towards political engagement, requires their support. The only sure way to secure such cooperation is to address the fundamental causes of Pakistan's insecurity, especially its latent and enduring conflict with India.

Source: *The sun in the sky: The relationship between Pakistan's ISI and Afghan insurgents* by Matt Waldman, Crisis States Discussion Papers 18, Development Studies Institute, London School of Economics, published June 2010.

Prevent the crime of silence

Bertrand Russell

Bertrand Russell founded The Spokesman. *We reprint his 1966 address in anticipation of the London session of the Russell Tribunal on Palestine which meets in November 2010.*

The first meeting of Members of the Vietnam War Crimes Tribunal, which took place in London on 13 November 1966, was addressed by Bertrand Russell. He was joined by Jean-Paul Sartre and the Italian jurist, Lelio Basso, among other notable men and women who were to give their time to hear the evidence presented to the Tribunal. The United States' war on Vietnam was to continue for several long years but, during the course of its sessions in Stockholm and Copenhagen (it was prevented from meeting in Paris), the Tribunal would make available eyewitness testimony of what was actually happening there.

In Rome in 1974, there followed a second Russell Tribunal, initiated by Lelio Basso, on Repression in Latin America. Russell had died in 1970, and it was his widow, Edith, who extended the initial invitations to those who agreed to serve in the investigations. After three sessions, a Permanent People's Tribunal was established, which continued its work in response to popular requests from many countries,

'There were many others who sought to emulate the Vietnam inquiries,' Ken Coates informed an international press conference in Brussels, in March 2009, which launched the Russell Tribunal on Palestine (see Spokesman 104*). One such initiative, in more recent times, was the World Tribunal on Iraq, with a truly global range of participants, which held its final session in Istanbul in June 2005.*

Now, the Russell Tribunal on Palestine will hold its second session in London from 20 to 22 November 2010. The London session will consider corporate complicity in Israel's violations of international human rights law and international humanitarian law. It follows an initial session in Barcelona in March, which found European Union Member States in breach of international and internal European Union law with respect to the protection of human rights of Palestinians (see Spokesman 108).

We reprint Russell's address of 1966, which resonates still.

*   *   *

Allow me to express my appreciation to you for your willingness to participate in this Tribunal. It has been convened so that we may investigate and assess the character of the United States' war in Vietnam.

The Tribunal has no clear historical precedent. The Nuremberg Tribunal, although concerned with designated war crimes, was possible because the victorious allied Powers compelled the vanquished to present their leaders for trial. Inevitably, the Nuremberg trials, supported as they were by state power, contained a strong element of *realpolitik*. Despite these inhibiting factors, which call in question certain of the Nuremberg procedures, the Nurernberg' Tribunal expressed the sense of outrage, which was virtually universal, at the crimes committed by the Nazis in Europe. Somehow, it was widely felt, there had to be criteria against which such actions could be judged, and according to which Nazi crimes could be condemned. Many felt it was morally necessary to record the full horror. It was hoped that a legal method could be devised, capable of coming to terms with the magnitude of Nazi crimes. These ill-defined but deeply felt sentiments surrounded the Nuremberg Tribunal.

Our own task is more difficult, but the same responsibility obtains. We do not represent any state power, nor can we compel the policy-makers responsible for crimes against the people of Vietnam to stand accused before us. We lack *force majeure*. The procedures of a trial are impossible to implement.

I believe that these apparent limitations are, in fact, virtues. We are free to conduct a solemn and historic investigation, uncompelled by reasons of state or other such obligations. Why is this war being fought in Vietnam? In whose interest is it being waged? We have, I am certain, an obligation to study these questions and to pronounce on them, after thorough investigation, for in doing so we can assist mankind in understanding why a small agrarian people have endured for more than twelve years the assault of the largest industrial power on earth, possessing the most developed and cruel military capacity.

I have prepared a paper, which I hope you will wish to read during your deliberations. It sets out a considerable number of reports from Western newspapers and such sources, giving an indication of the record of the United States in Vietnam. These reports should make it clear that we enter our inquiry with considerable *prima facie* evidence of crimes reported not by the victims but by media favourable to the policies responsible. I believe that we are justified in concluding that it is necessary to convene a solemn Tribunal, composed of men eminent not through their power, but through their intellectual and moral contribution to what we optimistically call 'human civilization'.

I feel certain that this Tribunal will perform an historic role if its investigation is exhaustive. We must record the truth in Vietnam. We must pass judgment on what we find to be the truth. We must warn of the consequences of this truth. We must, moreover, reject the view that only indifferent men are impartial men. We must repudiate the degenerate conception of individual intelligence, which confuses open minds with empty ones.

I hope that this Tribunal will select men who respect the truth and whose life's work bears witness to that respect. Such men will have feelings about the *prima facie* evidence of which I speak. No man unacquainted with this evidence through indifference has any claim to judge it.

I enjoin this Tribunal to select commissions for the purpose of dividing the areas of investigation and taking responsibility for their conduct, under the Tribunal's jurisdiction. I hope that teams of qualified investigators will be chosen to study in Vietnam the evidence of which we have witnessed only a small part. I should like to see the United States Government requested to present evidence in defence of its actions. The resistance of the National Liberation Front and of the Democratic Republic of Vietnam must also be assessed and placed in its true relation to the civilization we choose to uphold. We have about five months of work before us, before the full hearings, which have been planned for Paris.

As I reflect on this work, I cannot help thinking of the events of my life, because of the crimes I have seen and the hopes I have nurtured. I have lived through the Dreyfus Case and been party to the investigation of the crimes committed by King Leopold in the Congo. I can recall many wars. Much injustice has been recorded quietly during these decades. In my own experience I cannot discover a situation quite comparable. I cannot recall a people so tormented, yet so devoid of the failings of their tormentors. I do not know any other conflict in which the disparity in physical power was so vast. I have no memory of any people so enduring, or of any nation with a spirit of resistance so unquenchable.

I will not conceal from you the profundity of my admiration and passion for the people of Vietnam. I cannot relinquish the duty to judge what has been done to them because I have such feelings. Our mandate is to uncover and tell all. My conviction is that no greater tribute can be provided than an offer of the truth, born of intense and unyielding inquiry.

May this Tribunal prevent the crime of silence.

* * *

www.russelltribunalonpalestine.com

The Middle East

Free of nukes?

*Richard Falk
and David Krieger*

Richard Falk is the United Nations Special Rapporteur for the Palestinian Territories and chair of the Nuclear Age Peace Foundation. David Krieger is president of the Nuclear Age Peace Foundation.

Hardly a week goes by without an Israeli top official threatening to attack Iran so as to disrupt or destroy its nuclear programme, which is suspected of moving in the direction of acquiring nuclear weapons. Shamelessly, as well, the extreme right think-tanks in the Washington Beltway and many faithful followers of Israel echo these dangerous sentiments. They send Tel Aviv a signal that it has a green light to launch an attack on Iran at the time of its choosing, along with the reassuring message that the United States Government will step forward in support, whatever the adverse economic and diplomatic consequences for the region. True, there are occasional expressions of interest in continuing the search for a peaceful outcome coming from the White House, but the drift toward a military solution seems to be gathering an alarming momentum.

On the level of responsible international behaviour, it is disturbing because any non-defensive recourse to force violates international law and the UN Charter. Force is only lawful in international conflict situations if used as self-defence in response to a prior armed attack. The core Charter commitment in Article 2(4) prohibits threats as well as uses of force, and by that standard both Israel and the United States must be counted as law breakers. When the United States flaunts the Charter it was so instrumental in drafting after World War Two it sets a negative standard for others to follow.

On a more material level, there are a series of likely very heavy costs associated with carrying out an attack on Iran. Iranian leaders have a variety of instruments available for retaliation, and there is little reason to think that these would not be used. It is highly probable that Israel would be attacked in response by Hezbollah and Hamas, both of which have the capabilities to inflict serious damage. Even more damage could be done by Iran itself, which is developing long-range delivery capacities by way of advanced missile technology and a type of bomb-carrying drone aircraft. Then there exists the Iranian option to block passage through the Strait of Hormuz, through which two-thirds of the world's imported oil travels, undoubtedly producing supply shortages, a spike in prices, long petrol queues in countries around the world, and global economic chaos. Beyond this, there are a variety of unresolved conflicts in the region that could be easily inflamed by Iranian interventions, most obviously Iraq, and there remains the ominous possibility that the entire region would be transformed into a war zone.

What may be the most troubling aspect of this dreary picture is the failure to explore alternatives to the confrontational diplomacy, sanctions, and threat tactics so far relied upon to dissuade Iran from moving closer to the nuclear weapon threshold. The most attractive of these alternatives would be the attempted negotiation of a Middle East Nuclear Weapon-Free Zone. There is widespread awareness and support for this initiative among the governments in the region and the world. It was a priority goal agreed to by consensus at the 2010 Nuclear Non-Proliferation Treaty Review Conference. But there is one large catch that has so far been a decisive inhibitor: Israel is unalterably opposed, as the establishment of the zone would require Israel to dismantle its own nuclear weapons arsenal.

Obviously, the idea of a Middle East Nuclear Weapon-Free Zone has little regional appeal if it does not include Israel. Israel's insistence on retaining nuclear weapons while being ready to wage a war, with menacing repercussions, to prevent Iran from ever acquiring such weaponry, is expressive of the deeply troubling double standards that are an overall feature of the non-proliferation regime. When India went ahead and became an overt nuclear weapons state in 1998, it was rewarded by the United States rather than punished. The United States has directed much outrage at the allegedly undisclosed and officially denied Iranian nuclear ambitions over the years, but done its best to shield Israel from any criticism, or even from an obligation of full disclosure.

Such discriminatory nuclear diplomacy incurs high costs in the present global atmosphere of a questionable economic recovery and a stalled war in Afghanistan. The United States has so far been self-foreclosed from following the much more promising path of exploring the negotiability of a Middle East Nuclear Weapon-Free Zone that would immediately improve overall regional stability and, as well, take account of the prospect of many Arab countries poised to embark on nuclear energy programmes of their own. Indeed, without such a zone, there is a substantial possibility of a regional nuclear arms race that would tempt countries such as Turkey, Egypt, Syria, and Saudi Arabia, as well as Iran, to have the supposed deterrent benefits of a nuclear arsenal.

A Middle East Nuclear Weapon-Free Zone that includes all the countries of the region is an issue that demands US leadership. The stakes are high. It offers the United States an extraordinary opportunity to redeem its tarnished reputation in the region and regain its claim to provide responsible global leadership. Only the United States has the leverage and stature to bring the diverse cast of regional actors to the negotiating table to make the needed effort to avert war. There can be no advance assurances that such a diplomatic initiative would succeed, but to fail to try would be lamentable.

www.wagingpeace.org

What we have to do

Rep. Dennis Kucinich interviewed by Maya Schenwar

Dennis Kucinich was the only Democratic Presidential candidate who voted against the Iraq war authorization in 2002, and against every war-funding measure since. He has been warning for years that the Administration's belligerence towards Iran is unjustified. He represents the 10th District of Ohio in the United States House of Representatives. In Septemebr 2010, this unusual Congressman gave an exclusive interview to Truthout, one of the best sources of independent commentary and analysis in the US.

Maya Schenwar: *Since the end of formal combat operations in Iraq, you've been speaking out against the continuing presence of US troops and increasing presence of American mercenaries there. How do you respond to those who say the continued presence is necessary for security reasons?*

Dennis Kucinich: America's invasion of Iraq has made us less secure. Before the entire world we invaded a country that did not attack us – that had no intention or capability of attacking us – and that, famously, did not have weapons of mass destruction. The subsequent occupation has fuelled an insurgency, and as long as we have troops there, the insurgency will remain quite alive.

The very idea that somehow the war is in a new phase needs to be challenged. Insurgents don't differentiate between combat troops and non-combat troops; any of our troops who are out there are subject to attack. And the insurgencies will continue to build, with the continued American presence, resulting in the death of more innocent civilians.

Every mythology about our presence in Iraq is being stripped away. The idea that we can afford it? We can't. That Iraq will pay for it? It shouldn't and couldn't. That somehow we'd be welcomed there? By whom? That there's some kind of security to be gained in the region? We have destabilized the region. That it would help us gain support from moderates in the Muslim world? We are undermined throughout the Muslim world. Every single assertion of this war, and every reason for this war, has been knocked down. And yet it keeps going.

MS: *Then, is a complete, immediate withdrawal in order – right now?*

DK: That's what we have to do. We should have done it a long time ago. Is it likely that there will be conflict when we leave? Yes. We set in motion forces that are irrevocable. You cannot simply launch a war against a country where there were already factions – Sunnis, Shiites and Kurds who were at odds with each other – and think that you can leave there without difficulties. That's going to happen no matter what. But the fact that the conflict that we helped to create is still quite alive does not justify staying there. War becomes a self-fulfilling prophecy of continued war, unless you break the headlong momentum by getting out.

MS: Do you view Afghanistan similarly? Should we be looking at a quick, complete withdrawal?

DK: Well, Afghanistan is a separate war; it needs to be separated. I believe we were right to strike at al Qaeda immediately after 9/11. And I think most Americans believed that was the right thing to do. But it was wrong to invade and occupy the country. It showed an acute lack of understanding of history, and a lack of understanding of the people of Afghanistan.

At this point, Afghanistan has a kleptocracy. There's no remote possibility that it could sustain anything like a democratic system right now. And we have assured that by using US tax dollars to help prop up a bunch of crooks. When you think of the grotesque scene of Hamid Karzai being given the singular honour of a presence on the floor of United States Senate, and then you learn that some of the very people who are involved in corruption in Afghanistan were working with him on the CIA payroll, you know that what we've seen is a turn, not towards a *realpolitik* approach, but towards depravity masquerading as diplomacy.

We have lost our way through our misadventures in Iraq and Afghanistan, and we have to come home. Not only do we have to come home from Iraq and Afghanistan, but we also have to take a different look at America's presence in the rest of the world. Unless we start to focus on a global position for the United States that is not hegemonic, but is co-operative with international institutions, we're looking at nothing but one nightmare after another.

MS: *So, what do you think that new role in the world would look like for* *the United States? What would our position be if we made that shift?*

DK: We would start supporting structures of international law. With friend and foe alike, we'd support compliance with the Nuclear Non-Proliferation Treaty. With friend and foe alike, we'd support compliance with the Biological Weapons Convention and the Chemical Weapons Convention. And we'd submit to the fullness of those treaties. We'd support the small arms treaty, the landmine treaty. We'd support the United Nations. We would participate fully in an international criminal court.

Only when you have recognized global standards of justice can there truly be respect among nations. We cannot have one set of laws for the United States and another set of laws for the rest of the world. For example, our policy on claiming the right to pursue assassination anywhere we please: that is against everything America should stand for. And we haven't worked to craft a climate change agreement that is truly mindful of the environmental challenges we see – an agreement that would phase out coal and nuclear. The US is missing a historic opportunity to chart a new path in the world.

Let it be said, we have a right to defend ourselves. But we do not have a right to take international law in our own hands. We do not have a right to be police, prosecutor, judge, jury and executioner all in one fell swoop.

MS: What can the American people do right now if they want to effect change on the issues we're discussing?

DK: Support the candidates that support the change you want. We have an election coming up, and those candidates who really are dedicated to America taking a new role in the world, and taking care of things here at home, deserve support.

We need to ask candidates where they stand on these issues. If they voted to continue the war, will they go back to Congress and continue to support the war? People need to know that. Will they continue to vote for these appropriation funds? Will they continue to vote for resolutions that keep us at war? Will they continue to support the fiction that the 'global war on terror' has trumped Article I, Section 8 of the Constitution, with respect to Congress's role of declaring war in any country where the US has a military presence?

We all have to start thinking of national defence in a broader way. National defence should also mean a full-employment economy. National defence should mean jobs for all, health care for all, education for all, retirement security for all. We spend more on the military than every other nation in the world put together.

There's another thing we need to do in this discussion: we need to look at how we think of the world. If we see the world only as Us versus Them, as divided into warring camps, then our worldview produces an outcome which creates war. If we see the world only in terms of these dichotomies, that's a precursor of war. If we see a world where war is inevitable, that inevitability becomes a reality – we make it so.

But war is *not* inevitable. Peace is inevitable, if we are willing to explore the inherent truth of human unity – if we are willing to contemplate the undeniable fact that we're all one, that we are interdependent and interconnected. This compelling truth of human unity needs to be called upon at a time of division. It needs to be insisted upon. It needs to resound with the historical precedent of America's first motto, *e pluribus unum*: out of many, we are one.

I'm dedicated to continuing to work for an international policy where we work with the world community, where we use structures of international law and adhere to and participate in them, where we begin to understand that our role in the world cannot be as policeman of the world, and where we work with the nations of the world to achieve security for *all* people.

MS: *What would funding for non-violence look like?*

DK: We need to support a cabinet-level department of peace, which would serve to make non-violence an organizing principle of our society. The department would address issues of violence in our own society as well as head off war, through having somebody in the cabinet who could advise the President on non-violent conflict resolution. Funding would be pegged to 1 per cent of the Department of Defense's budget. One per cent! And that would be about $7 billion a year.

Why wouldn't we want to explore peaceful means of conflict resolution? We've explored war and war doesn't work. This is a different world. It's not World War Two anymore. There's a whole different technological structure to society. We can pick up a cell phone and call anyone, anywhere in the world; we can get on a plane and go anywhere in the world in half a day; we can send a text message anywhere in the world in seconds; we're already experiencing the world as one! Why aren't our social structures keeping pace? Why don't we demand that we come into rhythm with what is really an impulse towards unity?

Peace, which is achieved only through painstaking effort, doesn't have to cost a lot of money. We know what war costs. And it's not simply a matter of politicians doing it. Each one of us has to reflect on the way we look at the world and think about whether there's anything we do that contributes to violence, if there's anything we do that contributes to polarity. We really have to look at how the way we think is producing the particular kind of world we have. We could have the world any way we want it. We need to carefully analyse our own worldview to see if it's compatible with our survival.

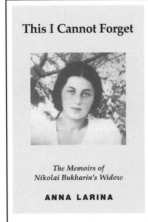

West Papua's Plight

Carmel Budiardjo

*The author writes on
behalf of TAPOL, a small
British-based organisation
which works to promote
human rights, peace and
democracy in
Indonesia. TAPOL means
political prisoner in
Indonesian. The
organisation was founded
in 1973 by Carmel
Budiardjo, herself a
former political prisoner
in Indonesia and Amnesty
International prisoner of
conscience.*

It is now more than ten years since the downfall of the autocrat Suharto when Indonesia was transformed from an authoritarian state into a country enjoying the trappings of democracy. But in the eastern provinces of Papua and West Papua, democracy is still a distant dream. The Papuan people are still mired in poverty, with malnutrition widespread among the children, and health and education facilities that fall far short of conditions in the rest of the country.

In 1969, when West Papua was still a single province, it was incorporated into Indonesia by virtue of a fraudulent Act of Free Choice which was neither free nor was there any choice.

Tribal chiefs representing just over one thousand people, acting under duress from the Indonesian military, voted unanimously in favour of incorporation into Indonesia. The UN shamefully 'took note' of this and West Papua was henceforth removed from the agenda of its decolonisation commission.

West Papua is richly endowed with natural resources which have attracted foreign investors like bees round a honey pot. They rake in huge profits while the Papuan people have never benefited from what is rightfully theirs.

From the very start, a US multinational was waiting in the wings. In a deal arranged personally by Suharto, the US mining giant, Freeport-McMoran, won a contract of work to exploit Papua's huge reserves of copper and gold in the central highlands. Villagers living in the mountainous area were required to leave their homes to make way for the concessionaire. They were forced to resettle in coastal regions, which resulted in a root-and-branch transformation in their way of life with grave consequences for their health and wellbeing.

Freeport has for many years been Indonesia's largest tax-payer, also paying dividends and other remittances to the central government. Just to give an idea of how profitable Freeport is, in the first quarter of 2010, it was able to double its dividend after recording a twenty-fold jump in profits.

According to the company's chief executive, Richard Adkerson, Freeport's operating cash flow totalled $1.8 billion, and he estimated that it would exceed $6 billion for the year 2010. Revenue for the company worldwide surged to $4.36 billion from $2.60 billion. He said that first quarter results reflected improved pricing as well as lower mining costs. The company's average realised price for copper was $3.42 a pound, as compared with $1.72 a year earlier, while the price of gold was 20 per cent higher.

In 2008, BP, a mainly British company, secured a deal to extract Papua's natural gas and began operations in Tangguh in 2009. The gas is extracted offshore in Bintuni Bay, causing disruption to fishing activities in the area. Papuans living along the north and south coast of the bay have been moved away, to make way for labour recruited from outside to work for Tangguh/BP.

These two foreign-owned extraction companies have led the way in a significant new influx of newcomers into West Papua.

West Papua has for many years felt the impact of major demographic transformation as a result of the transmigration programme launched back in the 1960s when Suharto was still in charge. Jayapura, the capital of West Papua, is now virtually an Indonesian city, with Indonesians dominating commercial activities and occupying many key posts in the provincial and local administrations. Visitors to Jayapura have been struck to see how Papuans traders, mostly women, only function on the fringes of the markets, selling their wares while seated on the ground in the open air, under the blazing sun.

Marginalisation of the Papuans

In the four decades since West Papua became a province of Indonesia, the indigenous people have gradually been overwhelmed by outsiders who now account for almost half the population, a trend that is set to continue as more and more projects are introduced. The biggest threat, at present, is a programme to convert large swathes of Papuan land into food producing estates, in the interest of securing food sufficiency for the country as a whole, with little regard for the rights of the indigenous Papuans who inhabit the land, and the preservation of their lifestyles, traditional culture and pursuits such as hunting and fishing that have, for centuries, catered to their basic needs.

The Merauke Integrated Food and Energy Estate – MIFEE – will cover 1.6 million hectares of land in the south-eastern corner of West Papua. Plots of land will be tilled by private companies, including some foreign companies, to grow food, using labour brought in from other parts of Indonesia. Estimates of the number of labourers likely to be employed to till the MIFEE plots vary hugely, ranging from just under 1 million to as many as 4 million.

The number of labourers will inevitably be augmented by wives and children, as this is not seasonal work and will result in the labourers settling in the area for years, if not for good. Some Papuan activists believe that MIFEE is only the first of several food-growing estates to be introduced over the coming years in West Papua.

There are dozens of Papuan political prisoners who are serving long sentences simply for unfurling their own flag, the Morning Star, at peaceful demonstrations in many parts of the territory. According to information from local non-governmental organisations, there are no fewer than 38 political prisoners, one of whom was given a sentence of 15 years for flying a flag. Another, who has just been released and who was arrested in 2004, also for peacefully flying a flag, was sentenced to ten years. The law granted Papuans a much greater say over the running of their economy and the use of money earned from the territory's highly profitable natural resources, as well as certain political rights that were previously denied, such as the right to set up their own political parties. One aim of the law was, undoubtedly, that, besides improving conditions for the Papuan people, it would hopefully persuade them to abandon their aspirations for independence, which had been denied them as a result of the fraudulent 1969 Act of Free Choice.

Over the years, however, special autonomy has brought about no meaningful improvements for the Papuan people; virtually all the stipulations in the special autonomy law have simply been ignored. For instance, the law provides for the creation of an all-Papuan assembly, known as the MRP, which must be consulted regarding government actions on social and cultural issues affecting the Papuan people. But when it was decided to split the province into two provinces, West Papua and Papua, no such consultation occurred. This decision resulted in the creation of new districts and sub-districts, and led to the influx of more Indonesian administrators. It has also led to the creation of new local military commands at every local administration, spreading troops more widely than ever.

In the past few months, the MRP has adopted a number of crucially important decisions, the most important being to 'hand back' the special autonomy law as a symbolic gesture of its rejection of the law. It also adopted eleven recommendations, including calling for a referendum on the issue of independence, for the demilitarisation of the territory, and for the Freeport to be closed down. Holding a referendum, which is a huge challenge to Jakarta, would mean restoring to the Papuan people the right to have a genuine act of free choice that was denied them so brutally in 1969.

Over the forty years of Indonesian occupation, the Papuan people have shown enormous restraint. Armed struggle has long since been abandoned in favour of what reverberates at every demonstration or meeting – for a Land of Peace in Papua. This is a call that must be heard round the world.

With grateful acknowledgements to Liberation journal.

We're not rats

Jimmy Reid

It was the speech that confirmed Jimmy Reid as the greatest Scottish orator of his time, and shaped the thinking of a generation of students. His Glasgow University rectorial address of 1972 was reprinted verbatim in The New York Times, *which described it as 'the greatest speech since President Lincoln's Gettysburg address'. That it resonates today is a tribute to its author, who died in August.*

Alienation is the precise and correctly applied word for describing the major social problem in Britain today. People feel alienated by society. In some intellectual circles it is treated almost as a new phenomenon. It has, however, been with us for years. What I believe is true is that today it is more widespread, more pervasive than ever before. Let me right at the outset define what I mean by alienation. It is the cry of men who feel themselves the victims of blind economic forces beyond their control. It's the frustration of ordinary people excluded from the processes of decision-making. The feeling of despair and hopelessness that pervades people who feel, with justification, that they have no real say in shaping or determining their own destinies.

Many may not have rationalised it. May not even understand, may not be able to articulate it. But they feel it. It therefore conditions and colours their social attitudes. Alienation expresses itself in different ways by different people. It is to be found in what our courts often describe as the criminal anti-social behaviour of a section of the community. It is expressed by those young people who want to opt out of society, by drop outs, the so-called maladjusted, those who seek to escape permanently from the reality of society through intoxicants and narcotics. Of course it would be wrong to say it was the sole reason for these things. But it is a much greater factor in all of them than is generally recognised.

Society, and its prevailing sense of values, leads to another form of alienation. It alienates some from humanity. It partially dehumanises some people, makes them insensitive, ruthless in their handling of fellow human beings, self-centred and grasping. The irony is, they are often considered normal and well adjusted. It is my sincere contention that anyone who can be totally adjusted to our society is in greater need of psychiatric analysis and treatment than anyone else.

They remind me of the character in the novel, *Catch 22*, the father of Major Major. He was a farmer in the American Midwest. He hated suggestions for things like Medicare, social services, unemployment benefits or civil rights. He was, however, an enthusiast for the agricultural policies that paid farmers for not bringing their fields under cultivation. From the money he got for not growing alfalfa he bought more land in order not to grow alfalfa. He became rich. Pilgrims came from all over the state to sit at his feet and learn how to be a successful non-grower of alfalfa. His philosophy was simple. The poor didn't work hard enough and so they were poor. He believed that the good Lord gave him two strong hands to grab as much as he could for himself. He is a comic figure. But think, have you not met his like here in Britain? Here in Scotland? I have.

It is easy and tempting to hate such people. However, it is wrong. They are as much products of society, and a consequence of that society, human alienation, as the poor drop out. They are losers. They have lost essential elements of our common humanity. Man is a social being. Real fulfilment for any person lies in service to his fellow men and women.

The big challenge to our civilisation is not *OZ*, a magazine I haven't even seen let alone read. Nor is it permissiveness, although I agree our society is too permissive. Any society which, for example, permits over one million people to be unemployed is far too permissive for my liking. Nor is it moral laxity in the narrow sense that this word is generally employed – although, in a sense, here we come nearer to the problem. It does involve morality, ethics, and our concept of human values. The challenge we face is that of rooting out anything and everything that distorts and devalues human relations. Let me give two examples from contemporary experience to illustrate the point.

Recently on television I saw an advert. The scene is a banquet. A gentleman is on his feet proposing a toast. His speech is full of phrases like 'this full-bodied specimen'. Sitting beside him is a young, buxom woman. The image she projects is not pompous but foolish. She is visibly preening herself, believing that she is the object of this bloke's eulogy. Then he concludes – 'and now I give ...' then a brand name of what used to be described as Empire Sherry. The woman is shattered, hurt and embarrassed. Then the laughter. Derisive and cruel laughter. The real point, of course, is this. In this charade, the viewers were obviously expected to identify, not with the victim, but with her tormentors.

The other illustration is the widespread, implicit acceptance of the concept and term, 'the rat race'. The picture it conjures up is one where we are scurrying around scrambling for position, trampling on others, back-stabbing, all in pursuit of personal success. Even genuinely intended friendly advice can sometimes take the form of someone saying to you, 'Listen, you look after number one'. Or as they say in London, 'Bang the bell, Jack, I'm on the bus'.

To the students I address this appeal. Reject these attitudes. Reject the values and false morality that underlie these attitudes. A rat race is for rats. We're not rats. We're human beings. Reject the insidious pressures in society that would blunt your critical faculties to all that is happening around you, that would caution silence in the face of injustice lest you jeopardise your chances of promotion and self-advancement. This is how it starts and before you know where you are, you're a fully paid-up member of the rat-pack. The price is too high. It entails the loss of your dignity and human spirit. Or as Christ put it, 'What doth it profit a man if he gain the whole world and suffer the loss of his soul?'

Profit is the sole criterion used by the establishment to evaluate economic activity. From the rat race to lame ducks. The vocabulary in vogue is a giveaway. It's more reminiscent of a human menagerie than human society. The power structures that have inevitably emerged from this approach threaten and undermine our hard-won democratic rights. The whole process is towards the centralisation and concentration of power in fewer and fewer hands. The facts are there for all who want to see. Giant monopoly companies and consortia dominate almost every branch of our economy. The men who wield effective control within these giants exercise a power over their fellow men which is frightening and is a negation of democracy.

Government by the people for the people becomes meaningless unless it includes major economic decision making by the people for the people. This is not simply an economic matter. In essence it is an ethical and moral question, for whoever takes the important economic decisions in society *ipso facto* determines the social priorities of that society. From the Olympian heights of an executive suite, in an atmosphere where your success is judged by the extent to which you can maximise profits, the overwhelming tendency must be to see people as units of production, as indices in your accountants' books.

To appreciate fully the inhumanity of this situation, you have to see the hurt and despair in the eyes of a man suddenly told he is redundant without provision made for suitable alternative employment, with the prospect in the west of Scotland, if he is in his late forties or fifties, of spending the rest of his life in the Labour Exchange. Someone, somewhere has decided he is unwanted, unneeded, and is to be thrown on the industrial scrap heap. From the very depth of my being, I challenge the right of any man or any group of men, in business or in government, to tell a fellow human being that he or she is expendable.

The concentration of power in the economic field is matched by the centralisation of decision-making in the political institutions of society. The power of Parliament has undoubtedly been eroded over past decades with more and more authority being invested in the Executive. The power of local authorities has been, and is being, systematically undermined. The only justification I can see for local government is as a counterbalance to the centralised character of national government.

Local government is to be restructured. What an opportunity, one would think, for decentralising as much power as possible back to local communities. Instead the proposals are for centralising local government. It's once again a blueprint for bureaucracy, not democracy. If these proposals are implemented, in a few years, when asked 'Where do you come from ?', I can reply: 'The Western Region'. It even sounds like a hospital board. It stretches from Oban to Girvan and eastwards to include most of the Glasgow conurbation. As in other matters, I must ask the politicians who favour these proposals — where and how in your calculations did you quantify the value of a community? Of a community life? Of a sense of belonging? Of the feeling of identification? These are rhetorical questions. I know the answer. Such human considerations do not feature in their thought processes.

Everything that is proposed from the establishment seems almost calculated to minimise the role of the people, to miniaturise man. I can understand how attractive this prospect must be to those at the top. Those of us who refuse to be pawns in their power game can be picked up by their bureaucratic tweezers and dropped in a filing cabinet under 'M' for malcontent or maladjusted. When you think of some of the high flats around us, it can hardly be an accident that they are as near as one could get to an architectural representation of a filing cabinet.

If modern technology requires greater and larger productive units, let's make our wealth producing resources and potential subject to public control and to social accountability. Let's gear our society to social need, not personal greed. Given such creative re-orientation of society, there is no doubt in my mind that in a few years we could eradicate in our country the scourge of poverty, the underprivileged, slums, and insecurity.

Even this is not enough. To measure social progress purely by material advance is not enough. Our aim must be the enrichment of the whole quality of life. It requires a social and cultural, or if you wish, a spiritual transformation of our country. A necessary part of this must be the restructuring of the institutions of government and, where necessary, the evolution of additional structures so as to involve the people in the decision-making processes of our society. The so-called experts will tell you that this would be cumbersome or marginally inefficient. I am prepared to sacrifice a margin of efficiency for the value of the people's participation. Anyway, in the longer term, I reject this argument.

To unleash the latent potential of our people requires that we give them responsibility. The untapped resources of the North Sea are as nothing compared to the untapped resources of our people, I am convinced that the great mass of our people go through life without even a glimmer of what they could have contributed to their fellow human beings. This is a personal tragedy. It's a social crime. The flowering of each individual's personality and talents is the pre-condition for everyone's development.

In this context education has a vital role to play. If automation and technology is accompanied, as it must be, with full employment, then the leisure time available to man will be enormously increased. If that is so, then our whole concept of education must change. The whole object must be to equip and educate people for life, not solely for work or a profession. The creative use of leisure, in communion with, and in service to our fellow human beings can and must become an important element in self-fulfilment.

Universities must be in the forefront of development, must meet social needs and not lag behind them. It is my earnest desire that this great University of Glasgow should be in the vanguard, initiating changes and setting the example for others to follow. Part of our educational process must be the involvement of all sections of the university on the governing bodies. The case for student representation is unanswerable. It is inevitable.

My conclusion is to reaffirm what I hope and certainly intend to be the spirit permeating this address. It's an affirmation of faith in humanity. All that is good in man's heritage involves recognition of our common humanity, an unashamed acknowledgement that man is good by nature. Burns expressed it in a poem that technically was not his best, yet captured the spirit.

In 'Why should we idly waste our prime', he writes:

The golden age, we'll then revive, each man shall be a brother,
In harmony we all shall live and till the earth together,
In virtue trained, enlightened youth shall move each fellow creature,
And time shall surely prove the truth that man is good by nature.

It's my belief that all the factors to make a practical reality of such a world are maturing now. I would like to think that our generation took mankind some way along the road towards this goal. It's a goal worth fighting for.

Is there not an alternative?

Michael Barratt Brown

Michael Barratt Brown is the founding principal of Northern College. His many books include Young Person's Guide to the Global Crisis and the Alternative *(Spokesman).*

To discover an alternative to the economic mess we are in, it is necessary first to consider the nature of the mess. This is just what Stephen Armstrong does in his book *The Super-rich Shall Inherit the Earth*, showing the way the new global oligarchs are taking over our world, that is in both developed and developing countries, and creating a vast gap between the super-rich owners and controllers of capital and the rest of us mere consumers driven deeper and deeper into debt. He starts with the so-called BRIC countries – Brazil, Russia, India and China. The obscene wealth of the Russian oligarchs is well known, but what is less well understood is the extent of support from the state, which has, not only in Russia but also in the other BRICs, made their super-riches possible. Armstrong avers that most of the Russian cabinet have seats on the boards of private corporations. The oligarchs, he maintains, are 'coming out of the recession well placed to act – a supportive state, better internal co-operation, and Western banks eager to help'.

The BRIC countries
It may seem surprising, perhaps, that London is where the super-rich from all over the world choose to live, until one realises what advantage the British tax system gives them. What is true of Russia is shown by Armstrong to be equally true of India, where, he quotes a former Indian senior civil servant writing that

'… a nexus has been established between a section of industrialists, a section of politicians and a section of bureaucrats. The principle of market forces guiding or dictating investments or of production targets being determined by demand and supply was given the go-by and everything was decided by administrative fiat.'

The best known Indian oligarch in the West, the world steel king Lakshmi Mittal, is said in India

'to be nothing. He is not one of the big five families – the families like Birla who bankrolled independence … you know how they made it; they kidnapped one of their main rivals.'

What about China? According to an experienced 'Chinese hand', quoted by Armstrong,

'the country is effectively run by some 100 to 200 families, who see the state's assets as their personal fiefdoms. They operate above the law – they're effectively untouchable … their sons and daughters are the Princelings, the children of senior Party officials.'

'So deeply interwoven are the Princelings and the super-rich,' Armstrong concludes, 'that holding out against a rapacious Chinese take-over can bring the full force of the state down on your head'.

And Brazil? 'Brazilian international expansion may not be treated with the same reverence as that of the three other BRIC countries, but it is beginning to become noticed,' says Armstrong. 'When it comes to Brazil's super-rich,' one oil man is quoted by Armstrong as commenting, 'the private sector effectively runs its own state'.

The super-rich in the developing world are not limited to the BRIC countries. They are well represented also in Africa, the poorest of all the continents, but having the widest gap between the few rich and the masses of poor. John Christensen, in his contribution to the *New Internationalist* collection, *People First Economics,* quotes the World Bank estimate that some $500 to $800 billions flow each year from poor countries to the rich, arising from criminal activities, corruption and tax evasion. This is five to eight times what was provided in aid to the poor by the rich. President Abacha of Nigeria had a personal fortune estimated at $5 billion to $8 billion salted away in the West, much of it in Switzerland. The Nigerian Education Minister suggested that the Swiss should top the list of the most corrupt nations for harbouring this loot. In my own book on Africa's trade, *Short Changed,* I cite the huge inequities of corporate transfer pricing and make the point that, in the much quoted examples of African corruption, one should look for the corruptor as well as the corrupted.

The US and UK Crises

John Plender, writing in the *Financial Times,* is quoted by Armstrong claiming that

> 'The financial élites in Washington and London more closely resemble the corrupt élites of Third World countries – with the main difference being that in the US the corruption is conducted in plain view while in the UK it is still hidden and furtive.'

The *New York Magazine* journalist, Joe Hagan, is quoted by Armstrong, writing of the fatal credit crunch weekend of 12th-13th September 2008, that he saw America's top bankers – from JP Morgan, Merrill Lynch, Citigroup, Credit Suisse, Morgan Stanley and Goldman Sachs – being driven into the basement of the Federal Reserve Bank. Other commentators have since asserted that US politicians do what the bankers want because they rely on them for their Parties' finances. Even Barack Obama, they say, 'dances to Goldman Sachs' tune'. Timothy Geithner, Obama's Treasury Secretary, and Larry Summers, from the Bush administration, are strong believers in Goldman Sachs bankers.

MIT professor Simon Johnson has expressed his fears over a US financial oligarchy – and the depths of Goldman's links with the heart of the US Government may seem thousands of miles away to the British – but Armstrong suggests that there is no reason to feel smug. In November 2009, the *Daily Mirror* listed the super-rich backers of the Conservative Party: including billionaire broker Michael Spencer, hedge fund magnates Stanley Fink and Michael Hintze. Next boss Simon Walker and textile heir Andrew Feldman donated over £3 million between them. Even more famously, the 'non-dom' Party Chairman, Lord Ashcroft, handed over £1.8 million, and pointed out that the cut in inheritance tax would be especially beneficial to the then '18 millionaire members of the shadow cabinet'.

It is an important fact of world finance, and the place of the super-rich in it, that most of the world's tax havens, where the rich can establish themselves to avoid paying taxes, are in British dependencies – Bermuda, Jersey, Cayman islands and Virgin islands. As one cynical, super-rich lady commented, 'only the little people pay taxes'. Rupert Murdoch is said to pay no taxes on his vast income. 'The problem', as Philip Augar, a former equities broker, told a conference at the London School of Economics in 2003, 'is that the influence of the City, the wealthy and business leaders reaches deep into the heart of pretty well every government'. The New Labour government cannot be excluded. Gordon Brown's leadership campaign was funded by private equity which, perhaps as a result, is exempt from normal company taxation.

Growing inequality everywhere

In 1986, according to the business magazine *Forbes,* there were 140 billionaires in the world. By 2008 the number reached 1,125, but dropped to 793 in 2009. Incomes everywhere grew between 1976 and 2006, but, according to Princeton Professor Raghuram Rajan, who was the International Monetary Fund's chief economist, more than half the growth went to 1 per cent of households in the US, making the country as unequal as it was before the Wall Street crash of 1929. Similarly, in the United Kingdom over the same period, according to the British analyst, Stewart Lansley, the top 10 per cent of earners saw their earnings rise 100 per cent, while those at the bottom rose by only 27 per cent. Such increasing inequalities are not only immoral; they are disastrous in their effect on the whole economy. Wilkinson and Pickett, in their book *The Spirit Level,* showed that in relation to a whole range of issues – mental and physical health, obesity, child pregnancy, longevity, crime and educational performance – more equal societies do better than the less equal. Their conclusions are reproduced in their chapter in the *New Internationalist* collection.

The effects of growing inequality are more serious even than that. Just as in the 1930s, increasing inequality can be shown to be the direct cause of the slump. This was the conclusion of J.K.Galbraith in his book *The Great Crash 1929*, which I referred to in my own 1999 study of *The Global Crisis* in arguing that increasing inequality was the major threat to the present economy. Raghuram Rajan was one of very few leading economists who foretold the coming of the 2008 crash, and accepts, with David Blanchflower, writing now in the *New Statesman,* that a double dip recession is the inevitable result to follow from the Coalition Government's proposed cuts in public spending and from the rehabilitation of the bankers. It was widely reported, in 2009, that Lord Mandelson had holidayed with Lord Rothschild on his Greek island, but less publicity was given to the fact that George Osborne, the new Tory Chancellor, was there too.

Tory policy, which combines cutting public spending and leaving the banks to replenish their assets, not only ensures a deepening of the recession, but its repetition in another decade or so. The clear insight of Keynes' analysis, that there was no natural level of full employment, to which economies will return, has been forgotten. Private capital investment in production depends on rising demand for goods. Even lowering rates of interest will not ensure new investment if there is not the demand in the economy for goods. Governments have to step in with public spending, best of all in capital projects, if economies are to be dug out of recession. Building pyramids would do, or arms orders, as in the 1930s, so long as men and women are set to work and start buying more goods. And this is just what is not happening under the current Coalition policies of public spending cuts. Rather the reverse.

Alternatives within a capitalist framework

It is a surprising fact, noted by Harry Shutt in his book *Beyond the Profits System*, that not one of the mainstream economists today is recommending the fundamental changes in the capitalist profit system, which were being considered in the last similar crisis in the 1930s. That is because of the subsequent failure of the Soviet system to achieve the alternative, better world that was promised in the 1930s. There is now a widespread belief among economists that 'sooner or later recovery will occur and the capitalist system – based on the pursuit of private profit maximisation – will be restored to health'. As recently as August 2010, John Redwood was claiming this in a BBC Newsnight television programme. But this really beggars belief, and runs contrary to all the lessons taught by Keynes in the 1930s. The decline in fixed capital investment in face of falling consumer demand, despite a previously unheard of rise in consumer debt and minimal interest rates, has led to the folly of increased speculation in a deregulated market. And not only to folly, but also to the criminality of much financial manipulation.

It is unfortunate for Kevin Doogan's *New Capitalism?* that the book was completed well before the economic crisis of 2007-8. There is only a brief preface, dated October 2008, which takes this into account, and his statistical tables end with 2002. For, while Doogan is critical of the free market trends of the previous three decades, and favours a return to a more regulated system, the purpose of the book is to demonstrate that it is not capitalism *per se*, in its latest globalised form, that is at fault, but the ideology of neo-liberalism. The major part of Doogan's study concerns the labour market. His statistical series between the 1980s and early 1990s do not show an increasingly precarious condition for labour, following rapid technological and demographic change and the globalising of the labour force as cheap labour from China and elsewhere has been introduced. This is supposedly the 'new capitalism' which gives the book its title and the question mark. Add another few years to the statistical tables, and the picture is much less hopeful. A minor point, perhaps, for any one deciding to read Doogan's book – they should be warned that, although it is said to be aimed at 'upper level' students, the sentence construction and length of words – such as 'exogenistical', 'transformationality', 'autonomisation' – are likely to put many readers off.

More importantly, even some of the writers with a much more critical stance than that of Kevin Doogan, those represented in the *New Internationalist* collection, see some possibility of recovery through greater financial regulation on an international scale, the taxing of bank profits, the reduction of bank size and the outlawing of tax havens, even a carbon tax and encouragement of private investment in 'green' energy, not to mention measures to support women, indigenous peoples and other marginalised consumers. Ann Pettifor of the New Economics Foundation makes not only her regular denunciation of the burden of debt hanging over developing countries, but also promotes the merits of the New Green Deal, which provides an alliance between the labour movement and the green movement. Most of the writers in this collection, however, and both Harry Shutt in his *Beyond the Profits System* and John Holloway in *Crack Capitalism*, go beyond mere regulation and amelioration to envisage a radical revolution in thought and practice that would end the determination of economic activity by the return to capital

Many of the authors under review see possible alternative directions and uses for economic growth, even within the capitalist framework – house insulation, wind turbines, heat and power systems, solar energy and other green measures. Several of the *New Internationalist* writers argue for such a switch, and there is no doubt that this would be possible even under capitalism. It does not appear, however, from what we can see of Tory Coalition policies in the United Kingdom, or even of the Obama Presidency proposals in the US, that this will happen. Coalition policies in the UK, as revealed in *The Guardian* newspaper of 14 August 2010, suggest the destruction of even those quite limited green measures that have been introduced by previous administrations up until now.

Alternatives beyond capitalism

Those who look beyond the limits of capitalism draw much encouragement for radical change from the evident collapse of the system in 2007-8 and subsequent failure of any signs of long-term recovery. This should be the moment for revolutionary change, they say. There are many suggestions in the *New Internationalist* collection. David Ransome, the *New Internationalist* editor, recalls that the G20 summit in London, on 2 April 2009, was met on the previous weekend by a demonstration of some

160 movements in Britain across the social and environmental divides, as well as by some direct action cracked down upon by the police leading to one death. This very large number of movements represented reveals one problem for revolution. Despite various attempts, there is no single unifying organisation or party of revolt in each nation state, let alone internationally. Similar protests have been recorded in other nation states. The nation state, as Ransome points out, remains the only institution with the necessary tax raising powers to take action, as was shown in the recent bail-outs. But it is combined international action that is required, and this is not even being supplied by capitalist governments, let alone by revolutionary movements.

All the alternatives that go beyond capitalism require some agency of change, and it is hard to see where that might come from. The strongest movements are the labour and green movements and the feminists, but movements for radical change are hard to organise and to keep going in times of crisis and unemployment. Most people are struggling then to keep their jobs, often in competition with fellow workers and with workers from other countries. Solidarity is hard to sustain in such conditions, and the special needs of women and excluded groups take second place. Strikes and labour unrest, protest marches and parades and other demonstrations of dissent, even mutinies, go so far, but require some leading force or uniting interest to take them into revolutionary activity.

Noam Chomsky, in his *New Internationalist* essay, sees hope for radical change coming from Latin America. Evo Morales, President of Bolivia since 2006, lays down a 'Ten Point Plan to save the world, life and humanity', which he presented to the UN. The points were principally directed to the problems raised by climate change, but they include an emotional appeal for unity in diversity, between white, brown, black and red, and much emphasis on the need for change to come from the bottom up rather than from the top down. This is in effect the central message of all the *New Internationalist* contributors, as well as that of Paul Shutt and John Holloway. The implications of this approach need to be examined closely.

When Harry Shutt comes half way through his book to propose a 'new model', he subtitles it 'ending the tyranny of production'. In this he includes the ending of the aim of what is called 'economic growth', which supposedly justifies the incentive of capitalist profit making. Economic growth has been shown to have grossly unequal results in income distribution and to be destroying the planet. Shutt's alternative model, like those of some of the other writers reviewed here, involves the development of social ownership and wide community partnership in decision making. The idea of expanding the commons is developed by Nicola Bullard and Derek Wall in the *New Internationalist* collection, just beginning with town planning, to provide for common space instead of private gardens, as Adiya Chakrborty has been proposing in his 'Brain Food' articles in *The Guardian*.

The question to be answered by all those who favour common ownership and popular control of the earth's resources and of human labour is where to begin. Co-operatives in both distribution and production get a brief mention, including the Co-operative Societies and the John Lewis Partnership in the UK, and *stadtwerke* in Germany, and the mutual savings institutions such as the UK's Nationwide Building Society. But these are comparative small fry in an ocean of big fish.

John Holloway, in his *Crack Capitalism,* starts from a fundamental critique of the way we live our lives. His thesis is that, however much we may hate the system, we create it all the time by allowing ourselves, albeit unwillingly, to be used as 'alienated' labour. He takes the term from Marx's analysis of capitalist production, in which labour is divided into useful or concrete labour and abstract or alienated labour, which the capitalist employs. Holloway develops the division to distinguish our doing things as a self-conscious satisfying activity and labouring in a way that alienates us from what we do.

A New Way of Living

How, then, can we move beyond alienation? Most of the *New Internationalist* writers make lists of what to do, but most of them are, in effect, negative – to stop doing what we are doing. George Monbiot has one really interesting positive suggestion, based on a number of experiments in different parts of the world, described by Bernard Leitaer in his book *The Future of Money.* All these experiments involved the use of an alternative money to that created as a monopoly by the central banks and then manipulated by the giant banking corporations. The most successful alternative currency systems include 'demurrage', that is a fee for keeping the money. In one such system the bank note has twelve spaces on it where you put a stamp each month to keep the note valid. After a year the note is withdrawn from circulation. As it becomes less valuable the longer you hold on to it, this encourages you to invest rather than hoard. Our obsession with money would be greatly reduced. Any scrip would do so long as it was widely trusted, and no organisation, public or private, could exercise monopoly.

Holloway suggests that there are cracks in capitalism to be exploited.

This is the meaning of the book's title. It is not purely hortatory but descriptive. Revolutionary activity consists in finding the cracks and seeking to open them up to enable us to develop more and more useful doing. In arguing for his thesis, Holloway rejects the idea of socialism as an alternative imposed by replacing the power of the owners of capital by the power of organised workers. That was the great error of Soviet planned economy. He is looking for a different way of living, with different social relations spreading from below up and not imposed from the top down. It will begin in the cracks in capitalism, where we can all find satisfying things to do with our neighbours and friends – community gardens, alternative radio stations, patient managed health centres, parent run schools, pensioner organised old people's homes.

Some of this sounds surprisingly like Mr Cameron's 'Big Society'. The main difference must lie in the possible sources of finance. Mr Cameron will certainly retain control of the funding, but Holloway's whole aim is to 'break the walls that close us', and that would start with the Treasury as well as with 'tyrant capital', as Holloway calls it. A fatal weakness in his book, however, is that Holloway never says anything about taxation and finance. Local taxation has lost its credibility as a result of local government corruption and the demands on the state in a globalised world economy. Suggestions that we should all be free to use our own money privately, just as we will, must suffer from the enormously unequal distribution of wealth. Some have proposed a state grant of a certain sum at birth for every child, to be invested securely and only redeemable after some twenty years. But such an invention of infant capitalists would hardly recommend itself to those trying, precisely, to free us from the capitalist system. We have to end this review of the economic alternatives with the sad conclusion that no one has yet come up with a complete answer, and we may have to concentrate on making the existing system more acceptable and on working away at our own several cracks in the system, to move towards a fairer and more sustainable world.

References

Stephen Armstrong, *The Super-rich Shall Inherit the Earth,* Constable, 256 pages, paperback ISBN 9781849010412, £8.99

David Ransome & Vanessa Baird*, People First Economics,* New Internationalist, 208 Pages, paperback ISBN 9781906523237, £9.99

Richard Wilkinson & Kate Pickert, *The Spirit Level: Why More Equal Societies Almost Always Do Better,* Penguin, 368 pages, paperback ISBN 9780141032368, £9.99

Raghuram Rajan, *Fault Lines: How Hidden Fractures Still Threaten the World Economy*, 272 pages. Princeton University Press, hardback ISBN 9780691146836, £18.95

J.K.Galbraith, *The Great Crash 1929,* Penguin, 240 pages, ISBN 9780141038254 (new edition), £9.99

Michael Barratt Brown, *Young Persons' Guide to the Global Crisis and the Alternative*, 128 Pages, Spokesman, paperback ISBN 9780851246208, £9

Kevin Doogan, *New Capitalism? The Transformation of Work*, Polity Press, 240 pages, paperback ISBN 9780745633251, £16.99

Harry Shutt, *Beyond the Profits System: Possibilities for a Post-Capitalist Era,* Zed Books, 144 pages, ISBN 9781848134171, £12.99

John Holloway, *Crack Capitalism*, Pluto Press, 272 pages, paperback ISBN 9780745330082, £17.99

Ken Coates – A subscriber writes

I never met Ken Coates, but I feel I knew him quite well. From the first, I was impressed by *The Spokesman* itself; always readable, even entertaining, and always informative (and there are not many 'political' publications about which that can be said). I was impressed, as I still am, by the high quality of the writing of its contributors and, of course, one of the best was Ken himself. His articles and editorials were masterpieces of clear, concise prose. They were hard-hitting as he expressed his anger and outrage at the injustices and cruelties of the world and what might be done about them. But he never 'preached' at you or lost his 'cool'. Rather, he seduced you round to his way of thinking – controlled anger is often far more effective than an ear-bashing, self righteous blast of rage. He is up there with the greats, alongside his friend, Kurt Vonnegut, George Orwell and Noam Chomsky.

There is a personal side to all this, of course. I once wrote to *The Spokesman* and was surprised to get a letter from the Editor, a real letter rather than a standardised one. I replied to Ken's reply, and was even more surprised when he replied to that. So began a reasonably regular correspondence. We discussed the problems of the world, but not just that. He showed interest in me, and told me a little about himself. His letters were witty, warm, generous, and full of humanity. I used to ask myself, 'How does he do it? Here is a man who mixes with the good and the great, who has many commitments, and he still finds time to write to me'.

I shall miss his letters and sending mine off to him.

Nigel Potter
Honduras

Act and Survive

An appreciation of Ken Coates

Stuart Holland

Stuart Holland's many books include Out of Crisis, The European Imperative, Towards a New Bretton Woods*, and* Full Employment for Europe *(with Ken Coates).*

Ken not only was the best of my friends for decades and also a key influence in my life. He was the only person I have known who combined intellectual and political genius with a formidable ability to mobilise others on alternative agendas. His self-direction was phenomenal, but fame was not the spur. Nor was there a single mind-set. Part of his genius was intuitive lateral thinking and 'coming up with' ideas that challenged convention, whether of the Right or Left.

One of these in which we were mutually involved, with Jacques Delors, was the case for a Social Europe, which, at present, is being lost rather than won, and may end in disintegration of the whole European project, unless progressive forces in Europe follow his example and jointly mobilise.

Another, conceived and then mobilised across Europe by him, was the Campaign for European Nuclear Disarmament. Someone skilled in such arts should edit the Wikipedia entry on this, which both ascribes the initiative to others and also claims that it failed. It did not fail in mobilising hundreds of thousands across Europe in opposition to Cruise missiles nor in gaining conviction that a Europe without intermediate range missiles could be a nuclear free security zone.

I drew on END in making this case to the Soviet leadership before Neil Kinnock's first visit to Moscow, and gained their agreement to a joint declaration by him and them that if a Labour government insisted that the US withdraw Cruise, they would not target Britain with SS20s and would agree to joint site inspection to confirm this.

They initially were sceptical of END since Edward Thompson had linked it with his 'exterminism' thesis, which they regarded as anti-Soviet, if not a CIA plot. But, after several hours, they accepted that case had credibility for Europe as a zone without intermediate missiles since withdrawal of Cruise also was supported by the SPD at a time when Cruise were deployed only in the UK, Germany and Italy. Within which there was implicit logic. If the governments of two of these three countries would insist on their withdrawal the third would be most likely to do so since, in terms of what Bruce Kent argued in relation to Libya in his earlier tribute to Ken (see *Spokesman 109*), the third country would not welcome being the only target.

Another Ken initiative was of less strategic importance, but entirely consistent with his concern for individuals rather than only for 'grand redesigns' and led to the release of Ahmed Ben Bella. This is recounted now in what can only be a very limited appreciation of Ken's significance, in which serendipity and the END appeal also played a key role.

In March 1980, he rang me in London to ask whether I realised that we were approaching the 15th anniversary of the coup against Ahmed Ben Bella by Boumedienne; that Ben Bella had never even been charged on any allegations of misconduct, far less crimes, had been in prison until about a year earlier and since then under house arrest at M'Sila on the edge of the Sahara. Of course I knew of the overthrow of Ben Bella but little of the rest. Ken added that the government had said that access to him was not resticted, but journalists were telling him that it was blocked.

With typical understatement, Ken asked 'Don't you think we should pay him a visit, perhaps with you taking an invitation from MPs for him to address them on how he now sees the future of the Third World?' As usual, he had prepared this well. Some of Ben Bella's former colleagues had suggested that on the 'the visit', if we got ourselves to Algiers, one of Ben Bella's former colleagues would drive us to M'Sila. They also advised that we should be prepared to get arrested.

Ken suggested that if we were so, he would simply claim that he could not speak anything but English. I would use French to insist that we had taken the government at its word that Ben Bella was 'at liberty', that if they detained us when I was a member of parliament bringing an invitation from others it would cause a poltical outcry, and that at worst we probably would be sent packing after we had delivered the invitation.

Getting the support of MPs was not difficult. During one division alone in the House I gained some 120 signatures for the invitation to him to come to London. For many of them the only surprise was that he was still alive. On timing, we chose a weekend. I would send a letter to the Algerian ambassador in London explaining that we would be bringing the invitation in person and of course counted on cooperation from the authorities.

*   *   *

But we posted it on the afternoon of Friday April 18th as we were leaving Heathrow for Algiers, reckoning that this either might reach a duty officer at the embassy on the Saturday, by which time we should be in M'Sila, or not be seen till the Monday, by which time officials in Algiers could confirm our claims with the letter to the ambassador. It also was convenient that my passport described me as a university teacher rather than a member of parliament. We should be able to get in even if there was some question on how we would get out.

On arriving in Algiers we were met by a former close colleague of Ben Bella's in government and a former commandant of the *Front de Libération Nationale* (FLN), Boussouf. He was short necked, thick knit, very muscular, and it seemed clear that, as later was said of Paddy Ashdown, he could kill a man with one blow. It also was more than probable that, during the liberation struggle, he had. In principle this was reassuring. We would be driven to and, hopefully, from M'Sila by a man who knew how to take care of himself. What should happen there was that we would arrive at the house in which he was detained at precisely 2.30 on the Saturday afternoon. He would already be stepping out of it and would accept the invitation from the MPs in the moments before we were arrested.

Slim, smiling and looking eminently presidential in a dark cashmere coat, Ben Bella walked down the steps. I gave him a copy of the early day motion and said to him in French that we would wish him to accept the invitation. He smiled and replied 'J'accepte, avec plaisir'. His wife Zahra, a former left wing critic of him in government, but who had married him in prison, wept with joy and embraced both Ken and me – as pandemonium broke lose.

While Ben Bella was descending the steps his government 'caretaker' was on a hand-held phone speaking volubly in Arabic and whose predictable logic soon was evident. Small troop carriers, which might have been Renaults or Russian, which was not our main concern at the time, but with troops with small arms and mounted machine guns, rushed to the house from lower down the street and placed themselves before and behind Boussouf's BMW. The officer in charge then said in French that we should get into the car and follow him. Ben Bella, knowing that we were prepared for this, renewed his thanks, smiled again and made a dignified return up the steps.

The short drive was to the prefecture of M'Sila. The French prefect system had been imposed on Algeria under colonial rule, and retained. But in a westernised Algeria, and on a Saturday, it was some time before the prefect could be found. We were separated into three rooms for questioning. In Boussouf's case it was an interrogation and he admitted thereafter that it had been 'hard'. In Ken's case it was a total failure since he beatifically responded in English to their questions that he did not understand a word that they were saying. In my case it prompted the response that they had detained a member of the British parliament acting on behalf of others and that there would be consequences for such a diplomatic and political error. As yet there was no explicit threat rather than evidence of confusion.

Then the prefect arrived and I was summoned to his office where he demanded, in French, what we were up to. I ran through our routine which was that the government had declared that the former and founding president of the republic was 'at liberty'; that we had taken its declaration seriously and sought to meet him. He then said 'who's behind this?' I passed him a copy of the early day motion with the invitation and signatures of the MPs to visit parliament to give us the benefit of his experience as one of the leading figures of the non-aligned movement with Nasser, Nkrumah, Sékou Touré and others, and his reflections now on issues of global development and governance. The prefect then asked 'who else?' To which I replied that, if Ben Bella were not seen to be free and also free to leave Algeria when and as he chose, there were hundreds more leading politicians and public figures across Europe who would condemn the Algerian government's claim that he was 'at liberty', and demand his freedom.

The response to his second question was mere aspiration. He paused and then said to me, 'Mr Holland, both you and I know perfectly well what you and Mr Coates are up to. You also probably realise that I have not as yet been able to gain a response to this incident from Algiers. But it is within my powers to require you to inform me of where you are staying in my country and also to require you both to remove yourselves from Algeria'. Where we were staying was of no signifiance since it was not with any supporter of Ben Bella, so I gave him the name of our hotel in Algiers, well aware that the security forces then might search it, but with no concern for what they might find, since it implicated no one. He than indicated that we were free to go, but must leave Algeria the next day. I said that I accepted this but that there would be consequences both from not allowing us access to Ben Bella and insisting on our extradition.

Ken, Boussouf and I then were re-united, which was when I asked Boussouf how it had been, and he admitted that it had been 'hard'. We were less elated than exhausted. We had got the invitation through to Ben Bella and he had accepted. I would report this to the MPs who had signed the early day motion. All seemed to be going well enough. Boussouf then started the long drive back to Algiers. It already was evening as he drove higher into the Atlas range.

I dozed off, while Ken was asleep already in the back seat. But I then woke up and observed that Boussouf was sweating, even though it was already night and the temperature was low. I asked him 'Boussouf, what's wrong?' 'Nothing' he replied. I went back to sleep yet then jerked awake when suddently he braked hard and asked him again. He repeated the same. Yet this time I persisted and said: 'Boussouf, we knew there was some risk in what we have been doing. But we also assessed the degree to which the regime itself would be exposed if it did not free Ben Bella. Why are you sweating now?' 'Because they cannot afford him to be free,' he replied. 'If he were free tomorrow this would destabilise the regime.'

The presumption was to be proved wrong. His freedom did not do so. But Boussouf than admitted to me that it was on such precipitous roads with no guard rails, as I had observed in the morning but without concern, that the FLN would 'front and back' French troop trucks by commandeered heavy lorries, then tip the trucks and troops into the chasms below. I chilled and stayed awake for some time. But then, again, fell back asleep. When we reached Algiers, Boussouf drove us to our hotel. We both expected our rooms to have been searched, to no avail. But then Ken called me from his. 'They've taken the END list,' he said.

This was a list of the good and the great who had signed the END Appeal, which Ken had drafted. He had showed it to me on the plane to Algiers. It was so early in the END initiative that it had no dedicated stationery. It was printed out on blank A4 pages. But it started with Austria, under which the first name was Bruno Kreisky. It ran through to Germany, on which the first name was Willy Brandt. Other heads of government or party leaders had signed it. It then came to Portugal, where the first signatory was Ramalho Eanes, much less well known but a former army general who at the time was president of the republic.

It was remarkable that the security people who checked our rooms either had not had the time to photocopy the list and return the original, or had not bothered. The difficulty in getting through to Algiers that the prefect at M'Sila had admitted seemed to have taken such time that our rooms had been checked only at a last minute.

But the 'lifting of the list' gave us the lead on what then happened. For the Algerian government decided to release Ben Bella from house arrest and allowed him to leave the country. What had been mere bluff by me in the encounter with the prefect in M'Sila about wider ranging support for his release appeared to have been confirmed by some of the most eminent politicians and personalities across Europe.

When he was freed, Ben Bella spent a short time in Paris, but then came to London. I was approached by a leading figure in the Arab League who told me that he and Zahra would wish to be guests at our home. Clearly there was no problem. We welcomed them and they slept in our unpalatial spare bedroom. Ken also joined us, with clearly good reason. Since what had happened at M'Sila, and its outcome, had been entirely due to him.

When with us, Ben Bella also made plain that, without Ken's initiative he still could have been at M'Sila, or elsewhere under house arrest, indefinitely. He paid tribute to Amnesty International, who had published multiple protests against his imprisonment and also then his house arrest, but added: 'They did well. They protested. But you acted.'

There then followed an event which was Ben Bella's first public appearance in the UK since his release, at the next Labour Party Conference. Understandably, it was packed, not least by many of the members of parliament who had signed the early day motion. Ben Bella spoke in French and I translated. But what he said was prescient rather than only retrospective.

Especially when a question was posed 'In prison you learned Arabic and read the Qur'an. Are you now an Islamist?' To which he responded, 'I am a Muslim first, an Arab second, and then an Algerian. I am also proud to be an African'. There then was a follow up question from the floor: 'And what of the Qur'an?' to which he responded. 'My friend, the Qur'an is the inspiration of our faith. It is not a Michelin guide to the 20th century'. From which now, in a new millennium, many might learn.

Reviews

Iraq: Deception and Cover-up

Brian Jones, *Failing Intelligence: The true story of how we were fooled into going to war in Iraq,* **bitebackpublishing, 332 pages, paperback ISBN 9781906447113, £9.99**

The Transport and General Workers' Union used to award the Frank Cousins Peace Prize. It was named in honour of the Union's distinguished General Secretary during the 1950s and '60s, who upheld the cause of peace and nuclear disarmament during the most dangerous years of the Cold War. Frank was described as the 'Awkward Warrior' by his biographer, Geoffrey Goodman. Awkward because he would not give in or stay quiet in the face of wrongdoing. A warrior, not because he was warlike, but because he took the struggle to those who would do down his members and their families and communities, and also to those who would, indeed, beat the drum for war.

'Awkward', in the sense described above, is the word that comes to mind whilst reading Brian Jones' account of the Iraq War, and his dissenting role in it. He has given us an extraordinarily important book, written by an insider who retained integrity whilst his superiors, and most of the politicians, compromised theirs.

Dr Jones goes back to the first Gulf War, in 1991, to establish the context for a long descent into war on Iraq. He identifies Clinton's Iraq Liberation Act of 1998 as indicative of long-term US policy to remove Saddam, years before 9/11. The attacks on New York and Washington in 2001 were to provide the opportunity to follow through on that policy.

In the second section of his book, entitled 'Deception', Dr Jones focuses on the period from early 2002 up to the beginning of the war, in March 2003. The 'Deception' in question is several fold. First of all, there is the Prime Minister's attempt to deceive the public into believing that, after 9/11, Saddam posed a real threat to his neighbours and the wider region, including British military bases in Cyprus, because of his supposed possession of weapons of mass destruction. 'Where's your evidence?' a sceptical public asked. Thus began the abortive attempts to win over public opinion to the coming war, which culminated in the publication of the dodgiest dossier, of September 2002, complete with the Prime Minister's harrowing Foreword.

But there was also another level of deception. This was within and around the 'intelligence community', of which Dr Jones was a long-serving member. In attempting to make a case for an unnecessary war, the Prime Minister called on the Joint Intelligence Committee, or JIC, to do much of the job for him. This was a complete subversion of the established role of the JIC, which was to provide the Prime Minister of the day with objective and measured assessments of perceived threats to the United Kingdom and its many interests. However, some senior intelligence personnel were ready to countenance such deceit, it seems, not least the JIC Chairman, John Scarlett, and the head of MI6, Richard Dearlove.

Perhaps they hadn't reckoned on awkward questions from the Defence Intelligence Staff (DIS) at the Ministry of Defence. As successive drafts of the September 2001 Dossier were circulated, Dr Jones and his colleague specialising in chemical warfare at the Nuclear, Chemical and Biological Weapons section of the DIS, which Jones headed, warned that the supposed intelligence about Iraq's weapons of mass destruction, and any threat they might pose, was misleadingly overstated. But their repeated warnings, about the spurious 45-minute period from instruction to launch of some chemical and biological battlefield weaponry and other key details, went unheeded by those drafting the dossier, who were closely attended by Alastair Campbell, the Prime Minister's press secretary. Then, at the last minute, MI6 remarkably turned up 'intelligence' about Iraq's production of biological and/or chemical agents, which Jones and his colleagues at DIS were not allowed to see. It 'confirmed' the Dossier's claims about Iraq's WMD. Dearlove briefed Blair about 'Report X' (X for unknown, as Jones has styled it, as he has not been allowed to see it). Report X would haunt the deceivers for years to come, even though it may have been with drawn as unreliable as early as December 2002!

As the Dossier was about to go to press, Dr Jones hastily put his objections in writing to his superior at the Defence Intelligence Staff. A more detailed written objection was also submitted, subsequently, by his colleague specialising in chemical weapons.

This was to no avail, or so it seemed at that time. The September dossier, soberly titled *Iraq's Weapons of Mass Destruction: The Assessment of the British Government*, was published to suitably sensational headlines such as '45 Minutes from Attack'. The UN's weapons inspectors returned to Iraq. In accordance with UN resolution 1441, Iraq submitted its declaration of what weapons and programmes it had. The early inspections found nothing, and Hans Blix gave reports to the UN Security Council about Iraq's varying level of co-operation with the inspections. In London, on one freezing Saturday in February 2003, millions of people brought

London to a halt in an attempt to avert the coming onslaught. But not enough MPs were listening, and Parliament duly failed to support an amendment which sought simply to give the inspectors more time to complete their work. In truth, the countdown to shock and awe on Iraq had started in earnest in summer 2002, and the Bush Administration was not to be deprived of its war by a tidal wave of public opposition in Britain. Nor was Mr Blair.

Was there a measure of self-deception on the part of Bush and Blair? Probably. Certainly, there was growing consternation at the top as the occupiers spread out across Iraq, but no weapons of mass destruction were found. 'Give it time,' we were told, but quite soon the cover-up of the deception (that there was substantial intelligence about Iraq's WMD) was in full swing. The Defence Intelligence Staff memos were to prove central to exposing the cover-up of the deception, which forms the third section of Dr Jones' narrative, though this is only now becoming clear due to the publication of this most valuable book.

In his conclusions, Dr Jones proposes major organisational change for the intelligence services. He does not discuss the advent of the United Kingdom's National Security Council, ushered in with the arrival of the Coalition Government (see Spokesman 109). Some of us question the utility of many of these functions, which are unaccountable, undemocratic, and very costly. They closely bind the United Kingdom into the foreign policy priorities of the United States. But that is a wider discussion. For the moment, we celebrate the publication of *Failing Intelligence*, which is a genuine blow for freedom.

Tony Simpson

Chomsky

Jean Bricmont and Julie Franck (editors), Chomsky Notebook, Columbia University Press, 360 pages, paperback ISBN 9780231144759, £20.50. Originally published in French in 2007.

As a linguist, my interest in reading *Chomsky Notebook* came from a knowledge of the subject's contributions to the realms of language acquisition and generative grammar. Anyone involved in this field knows the unparalleled esteem in which Noam Chomsky is regarded, and his work over the last 50 years has formed the basis of much important linguistic theory and research.

The first thing to note about the *Chomsky Notebook*, therefore, is the relative lack of attention paid to linguistics. As a collection of works by different authors (including two by Chomsky himself) there are just three articles devoted to linguistics – Boeckx and Hornstein's review of the development of generative linguistics in general, Chierchia's exploration of 'Language, Thought and Reality After Chomsky' and Grodzinsky's quite advanced exploration of how generative syntax relates to brain function. Most of the book provides a whistle stop tour of some of Chomsky's other interests.

Herein lies both the strength and the downfall of this book. An overview of Chomsky's political engagements – particularly America's involvement in Vietnam and, more recently, Afghanistan – was welcome. However, when discussing education, nature and the media, the information was frequently second-hand – 'influenced' by Chomsky rather than dealing with his own actual contributions – or pitched at a very high level. 'Linguistic Theory and Language Processes' was, for me, the most interesting section, but how accessible would it be to anyone who hasn't a fairly high level of linguistic training? As an introduction to Chomsky's many and varied areas of academic involvement, this is a challenging and useful collection, but I recommend choosing articles of particular relevance or interest, rather than tackling the book as a whole.

The chapter on 'Chomsky and the University' by Pierre Guerlain provides an interesting, though perhaps unintentional, suggestion that such a dichotomy might be applied to Chomsky himself. Guerlain proposes that, too often, Chomsky has been attacked, misquoted or misrepresented in the media or in academic circles because of his involvement in a wide range of fields. Despite the fact that he has probably read more and formed more balanced and intelligent opinions than most academics in their chosen fields, it is suggested that Chomsky is often marginalised on the grounds that he is viewed distrustfully – especially with regards to his involvement in politics. The eternal problem facing his critics is that Professor Chomsky is unquestionably regarded as one of the most influential scholars in linguistics, so his opinion on any matter carries a deserved credence.

The interview with Chomsky, conducted by one of the editors, is a fascinating snapshot of this in action. Several times Chomsky corrects points of view that have been incorrectly attributed to him, or clarifies material produced by him that has been taken out of context. The overriding impression from the interview, and the book as a whole, is that he spends a lot of time having to do just that.

Gareth Carrol

Curious scholarship

Patrick J McDonald, *The Invisible Hand of Peace,* **Cambridge University Press, 352 pages, hardback ISBN 9780521761369, £45, paperback ISBN 9780521744126, £16.99**

A publisher's introduction states that

> *The Invisible Hand of Peace* shows that the domestic institutions associated with capitalism, namely private property and competitive market structures, have promoted peace between states over the past two centuries. It employs a wide range of historical and statistical evidence to illustrate both the broad applicability of these claims and their capacity to generate new explanations of critical historical events …

A promise of peace delivered invisibly, and almost inevitably, has to be taken seriously and examined further. When I had read no further than page 13, I was satisfied that this was not an unconditional offer. One large imposed condition was that of capitalism with competitive markets structured in a very particular way. To explain this the author, an Assistant Professor in the Department of Government at the University of Texas at Austin, (later described as 'Professor McDonald') quotes F A Hayek (1899-1992) in *The Road to Serfdom* (1944 and 1994 editions, University of Chicago Press):

> If 'capitalism' means here a competitive system based on free disposal of private property, it is far more important to realise that only with this system is democracy possible

and the author goes on to say

> This possibility suggests that the peace observed between democratic states may be caused by the tendency to possess relatively liberal market institutions rather than their embrace of open political competition in elections.

First we have to examine the meaning of *free disposal of private property.* To be free to dispose of it one must be sure that one has not already lost it by taxation, for example, or that one's disposal to beneficiaries will not be impaired by inheritance tax. Economists of the Chicago School care a great deal about taxation, and they would surely not be so careless as to confuse free disposal of private property with disposal only of such residues of wealth as might remain after taxation. So one of the essential conditions, not only for democracy, believe it or not, but also for the success of *the invisible hand* is that there be no taxation of private property. The law describes companies as persons. Would the government have enough money to conduct elections? Or to start a war? Perhaps not quite what the author had in mind.

It is hard to take such arguments seriously when one recalls the effects of Hayek's influence in Chile. Friedrich Hayek's tenure as a professor at the University of Chicago predated the recognition of the Chicago School of Economics under Milton Friedman, whose economic liberalism also enjoys the endorsement of the author and some right wing western leaders. Hayek was invited to the White House to advise President Ronald Reagan, in 1988, and he was awarded the Presidential Medal of Freedom by George H W Bush in 1991. He visited Chile several times in the 1970s and 1980s, during the dictatorship of General Pinochet and, in translation, was attributed the statement

> Personally I prefer a liberal dictator to democratic government lacking liberalism.

He wrote to *The Times* of London with the opinion that

> Personal freedom was greater under Pinochet than it had been under Allende.

and he recommended liberal economic reforms for Britain to Mrs Thatcher. In the late 1970s, she endorsed Hayek's book, *The Constitution of Liberty,* saying 'This is what we believe'. She befriended Pinochet when he was under arrest in Britain on the application of a Spanish judge citing human rights violations.

Military dictatorship in Chile was formed in 1973 under Pinochet, with United States gunboats offshore and other assistance from the USA. The democratically elected President Allende was confined, and died when the Presidential Palace was bombarded. Thousands more supporters of democracy were imprisoned, tortured or never heard of again. So much for free market freedom and democracy.

Democracy and peace are not to be so easily conflated either. In fairness, the author has not, so far as I read, attempted it. A democracy such as the United States, which spends a trillion dollars annually on weapons and maintains more than 700 military bases in more than 120 countries abroad, can hardly be peaceful. Nor has it been.

I paused before reading more of this book with such curious scholarship. If it has value, it is the caution that its extremism invites for the UK Coalition Government's free market and small government policies. I turned to Naomi Klein's *Disaster Capitalism,* and found it more convincing.

Christopher Gifford

Cruelty

Medical Justice, *'State Sponsored Cruelty'*: *Children in immigration detention (Summary Report)*, 16 pages

Since early 2009, I have been in correspondence with the Home Office regarding the detention of children at Yarl's Wood Immigration Removal Centre. In nearly all the communications I was assured that 'the welfare of children is a primary concern of the UK Borders Agency', but never was there any mention that this draconian practice was to end. So when, in July 2010, Nick Clegg stated at Prime Minister's Questions that he could 'confirm that the Government will come forward shortly with an announcement about how we will deliver on our pledge to end child detention and to close the Yarl's Wood Detention Centre for good', I was delighted.

This elation was short lived. I received a copy of *'State Sponsored Cruelty': Children in immigration detention (Summary Report)* by Medical Justice and was horrified to read there have been a 'number of reports that children have continued to be detained' at Yarl's Wood, including a child still in detention as the report was being published on 5th September 2010. I read through the 16 pages with a heavy heart.

In 2001, the New Labour Government decided to detain families for the purposes of immigration in the same way that they were detaining individual adults. So, for nine years the custom of locking up children in one of the three detention facilities around the UK has been practised. What is fortunate, however, is that it hasn't gone unnoticed. Medical Justice, the 11 Million Campaign, OutCry!, and End Child Detention Now (to name a small number of non-governmental organisations in this field) have carried out detailed investigations into the effects of detention on children and their families.

The key findings of this summary report are based on the cases of 141 children from 87 families who were detained between 2004 and April 2010. Amongst them, 74 children had psychological impairment as a result of detention, symptoms including bed wetting, anxiety, food refusal and panic attacks; 61 children said they were arrested in dawn raids and 44 of them later developed behavioural changes as a result, with six of them reporting the use of excessive violence during these raids; 92 children had physical health conditions that were made worse or caused by immigration detention, but they didn't receive appropriate medical attention for their condition.

Each case study in this report, and all the others like it, describe nightmare scenarios where children and their families are treated without little apparent regard to the fact that they are human beings. In the majority of cases the adults have fled countries where they have experienced torture, rape and mutilation, and they worry about being sent back for fear of reprisals. A number of the women in detention have suffered female genital mutilation and do not want their daughters, who were born in the UK in most cases, to undergo this barbaric practice.

If the Coalition Government wants to change the country for the good, as it repeatedly claims it does, then it needs to end the detention of children for immigration purposes with immediate effect. On 10th June, the United Kingdom Border Agency sent a letter stating that there would be a 'review' by David Wood, the director of criminality and detention for UKBA, into ending the detention of children that would run until the 13th July 2010, and that the findings would be made public. So far, Medical Justice reports, no findings have been made public and there have been no further announcements from the government. *'State Sponsored Cruelty'* – *Children in immigration detention (Summary Report)* calls on the

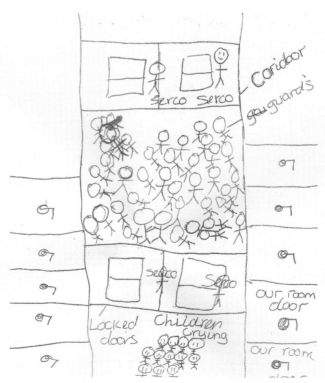

A child's picture of life inside Yarl's Wood

Coalition Government to live up to their 'potentially positive' pledge by decommissioning Immigration and Removal Centres before 1st December 2010. I add to this recommendation by suggesting to Nick Clegg he would do well to keep in mind Bertrand Russell's appeal to 'remember your humanity and forget the rest'.

Abi Rhodes

The full 84-page report may be downloaded
(http://www.medicaljustice.org.uk/content/view/1420/89/)

Americas

Grace Livingstone, *America's Backyard: The United States and Latin America from the Monroe Doctrine to the War on Terror*, Zed Books, 256 pages, paperback ISBN 9781848132146, £19.99

All those committed to Britain's 'special relationship' with America, on the grounds that it is the major force for democracy in the world, should read this book, which surveys US policy towards Latin America from the Monroe Doctrine of 1823 to the edicts of President George W. Bush. It's a record of gross bullying, the undermining of progressive governments, military interventions, the training of repressive armed forces, support for military coups and the backing of privileged oligarchies and American business interests against the elementary rights of the mass of the population.

Between 1898 and 1934 alone, the United States sent its armed forces into Costa Rica, Guatemala and Haiti once; into Panama twice; into Cuba, the Dominican Republic, Mexico and Nicaragua four times; and into Honduras seven times.

After 1945, in the name if containing communism, America supported and, in some cases, aided the advent to power of military juntas and ruthless dictators. It trained their forces and conspired – particularly through the CIA – to destabilise unco-operative governments.

When, in 1954, a progressive president in Guatemala, Jacobo Arbenz, sought to take over uncultivated lands from its largest landowner, the American company, United Fruit, and others, President Eisenhower authorised the CIA to remove him. An army of Guatemalan exiles under a disaffected officer, Carlos Castillo Armas, was recruited and trained in order to invade. Arbenz was overthrown and a 36 year long civil war was initiated, leading to the deaths of 200,000 Guatemalans.

When the Cuban dictator, Fulgencio Batista, was overthrown by a guerrilla army led by Fidel Castro, in 1959, as soon as the new government enacted policies to take over lands and enterprises owned by Americans, President Eisenhower approved a campaign to oust it. As Castro countered US measures to hit the Cuban economy by agreeing to sell sugar to the USSR in return for Soviet oil, and nationalised the refineries when they refused to refine it, the CIA organised an army of dissidents to invade. However, the invaders were defeated at the Bay of Pigs in 1961, leading to an even tougher embargo and other efforts to overthrow the regime which have continued up to the present time.

Having lost this endeavour, the US launched the Alliance for Progress, which purported to aim at reform but poured military and other aid into Latin America and trained thousands of soldiers in methods of neutralising rebels. This included the use of fear, payment of bounties for enemy dead, beatings, false imprisonment, executions and use of truth serum, according to manuals quoted by Grace Livingstone [p.41].

After 1961, a series of right wing military coups occurred, which the US helped to engineer or subsequently supported. In the Dominican Republic, the dictator Rafael Trujillo was overthrown by a coup in 1961, but when a progressive president, Juan Bosch, was elected and ousted, President Lyndon Johnson sent in American troops to prevent him regaining office.

In Brazil, the populist president Joao Goulart was the victim of a military coup in 1964. In Argentina there were several unconstitutional changes of ruler until, in 1976, Isabel Peron, the widow of former president Juan Peron, was removed from office by an utterly ruthless military junta under General Jorge Videla. This organised the torture and 'disappearance' of many thousands of people suspected of opposing it. Some were thrown out of helicopters into the Atlantic Ocean. A vicious dictatorship was also established in Uruguay.

In Chile, the CIA worked for years to prevent the election of Salvador Allende, a socialist, as president. When he eventually won in 1970, US President Richard Nixon, Secretary of State Henry Kissinger, and CIA Director Richard Helms conspired to remove him. His chief of staff, General René Schneider, was assassinated and the CIA then secretly helped prepare the ground for his successor, General Augusto Pinochet, to launch a military coup in August 1973. This succeeded and resulted in barbaric repression and thousands of deaths, but the new regime was swiftly recognised by the US.

In Central America, the US administration sought to prevent the victory of the Sandinistas against the Somoza dictatorship and its successors in

Nicaragua. In El Salvador, it backed the fourteen families and the ruling oligarchy against the Frente Farobundo Marti, leading to the assassination of Archbishop Romero in March 1980 and mass murders by death squads organised by Roberto D'Aubuisson who, in 1981, founded the right wing Arena party.

President Jimmy Carter did try to moderate the hardline US policies, but his secretary of state, Zbigniew Brzezinski, largely frustrated this. When President Ronald Reagan was elected, support for reactionary, undemocratic governments and movements knew no limits.

Despite this, the dictatorships in Argentina, Brazil and Chile came to an end in the 1980s and peace agreements were eventually made to conclude the civil wars in Central America. The 1980s and 1990s were lost decades for Latin America as a result of the neo-liberal policies implemented by the right wing governments with US support. Poverty and inequality soared.

This trend was, however, gradually reversed by the subsequent advent to power of more left wing governments which, to a greater or lesser extent, moved away from neo-liberalism and unmitigated free market economics. With the victories of Hugo Chavez in Venezuela, Luis Ignacio da Silva (Lula) in Brazil, moderate progressives in Chile, Evo Morales in Bolivia, Raphael Correa in Ecuador, Fernando Lugo in Paraguay, the Kirchners in Argentina and Daniel Ortega in Nicaragua, the Latin American scene was transformed.

American policy, however, did not change. Even President Bill Clinton – apart from support for a short-lived restoration of Jean Bertrand Aristide in Haiti – remained committed to traditional right wing US policies. The Torricelli and Helms Burton Acts sought to tighten the embargo on Cuba, and the North Atlantic Free Trade Area was promoted, with adverse effects on numerous aspects of Latin American economies.

Upon his election, President George W. Bush appointed ultra right wing officials like Paul Wolfowitz, Dick Cheney, John Bolton and Donald Rumsfeld to direct policy.

In making this carefully researched study of American policy in Latin America, Grace Livingstone has produced an invaluable book which should be purchased, read and kept for reference by all who wish to obtain a true picture of Latin American affairs. Hopefully, the peak of US domination of the continent has passed, but it is high time that the enormities of American imperialism throughout the region were more generally known and fully recognised. This text is an important contribution towards this end.

Stan Newens

Bloodbaths

Edward S. Herman and David Peterson, *The Politics of Genocide*, **Monthly Review Press, 160 pages, ISBN 9781583672129, £10.95**

Distorting and manipulating the truth for popular consumption is, of course, an important element in sustaining the power élite's control over the public psyche, and for the United States and the United Kingdom it is particularly important at present, given their active military role and consequent martial fatalities. It is a process which Noam Chomsky and one of the co-authors referred to as 'manufacturing consent', and it is therefore altogether fitting that Chomsky should have contributed the foreword to this important book.

The Politics of Genocide is firmly written in the tradition of Chomsky and Herman's 'Propaganda Model', and defines the bloodbaths into four 'partly ironic and partly serious' categories: 'constructive, benign, nefarious and mythical (the latter a sub-category under nefarious)'. With 29 'extremely serious' military interventions since 1945, the United States has need of a pliant media to explain its warlike hyperactivity, and this book seeks to expose the lies, double standards, obfuscations and the total failure to mention uncomfortable contradictory facts practised by the US media and politicians.

The categorisation of the bloodbaths will be clearer with examples, so under 'constructive' are the Iraq sanctions regime and the subsequent invasion, which were carried out by the United States and its allies for particular reasons associated with its direct immediate interests. The text catalogues the terrible price these two 'bloodbaths' have exacted on the Iraqi people, including over 500,000 sanctions-related child deaths. The approach of the US media to these events is carefully analysed: a table of newspaper usage of the word 'genocide' reveals that economic sanctions on Iraq resulted in 80 such references, and yet there were 323 relating to Kosovo, 1,172 to Darfur, and 3,199 to Rwanda. The economic sanctions levelled on Iraq, the authors are convinced, were the worst atrocity in 30 years. Madeline Albright, we recall, made the statement that the 500,000 early child deaths was a price 'worth paying'.

The 'nefarious' outrages encompass Darfur, Kosovo and Rwanda. These are events targeted by the US because they are associated with nations such as Sudan and Serbia, which have fallen foul of US concerns. Darfur, for example, presses many of the right buttons for Western and US interests – Chinese economic penetration, a supposed fundamentalist light-skinned Muslim Arab government pitted against black African Christian herdsmen. In fact, most of the population of Sudan is of the same skin colour, including Darfur. The major cause of the conflict is not religion nor tribalism, but a changed environmental situation, most likely caused by global warming.

The events in Rwanda, as portrayed here, espouse a completely different narrative from that provided by the media, which has concentrated on the Hutu killings, giving little insight into the motives of the participants besides tribal rivalry. Herman and Peterson accuse Kagame, leader of the *Rwanda Patriotic Front* and now Prime Minister, together with the Ugandan President Museveni and the US and other European states of conspiring to destabilise Rwanda by provoking mass murder, all in the interests of grabbing the mineral wealth of the Democratic Republic of Congo, the adjacent utterly chaotic traumatised giant which over the last few years has endured upwards of five million civilian deaths, according to some experts. The book does an excellent job in exposing the duplicity of the media and politicians in a searing investigation that makes the inexplicable make sense. The authors have scrupulously established the connections between those involved in the geopolitics of the region and its great prize: the vast mineral wealth of the Democratic Republic of Congo where Ugandan and Rwandan troops have been active.

The 'benign genocides' are massacres carried out by the nations aligned with the US, which need to be minimised, ignored or explained away. Afghanistan, El Salvador, Croatia's Operation Storm, East Timor all get a mention, and the book includes the Israeli's recent invasion of Gaza and the horrific massacres at the Sabra and Shatila refugee camps in Beirut in 1982. The final analysis is of the 'mythic' massacre in Kosovo at Racak, which provided a 'war justification' for NATO's bombardment of Serbia.

The International Criminal Court, established in July 2002, also comes in for criticism from the authors, who note in passing that the Court has so far been able to indict only black Africans from three countries. No Court action has been taken over Iraq, a blatant case of aggression and, to avoid embarrassment, the United States has revoked its signing of the Rome Statute which set up the Court's parameters. These parameters include the crime of genocide, crimes against humanity, war crimes and the crime of aggression. The latter crime of aggression is not operable by the Court owing to an inability to define what actually constitutes aggression!

The authors have performed a vital task in gathering together, and meticulously using, the data to show the bias, double standards and manipulation practised by the media, all in the cause of providing a smokescreen to disguise the real intentions of American foreign policy. *The Politics of Genocide* is concise, well documented and an important contribution to providing a uniform standard for judgments on human rights. It deserves to become a classic of its kind, endorsing the dictum of George Orwell, 'in a time of deceit telling the truth is a revolutionary act'.

John Daniels